STANDARD GRADE

Business Management

course notes **2nd edition**

Cover design by Caleb Rutherford

02/120508

ISBN 978-1-84372-490-2

Published by
Leckie & Leckie Ltd, 3rd Floor, 4 Queen Street, Edinburgh EH2 1JE
Phone: 0131 220 6831   Fax: 0131 225 9987
enquiries@leckieandleckie.co.uk www.leckieandleckie.co.uk

Special thanks to
Project One Publishing Solutions, Edinburgh (Project management and editing)
The Partnership Publishing Solutions (Design and page layout)
Ellustration (illustrations)

A CIP Catalogue record for this book is available from the British Library.

Leckie & Leckie is a division of Huveaux PLC

Acknowledgements
Leckie & Leckie has made every effort to trace all copyright holders. If any have been inadvertently overlooked, we will be pleased to make the necessary arrangements. We would like to thank the following companies/individuals for generously giving permission to reproduce their copyright material free of charge:
Arnold Clark; Alton Towers; McCallum Bagpipes; Nestlé; Peckham's; Peter Devlin (photographer) and the Scottish SPCA; Rangers FC; Stitch Master; Stoats Porridge Bars; Tesco.

CONTENTS

INTRODUCTION

It is impossible to cover a 2-year course completely in 112 pages. If, however, you work through these *Course Notes* and answer the questions and do the internet tasks you will have covered a lot. The book covers course content at Foundation, General and Credit levels, and apart from the sections highlighted as Credit material, the content is suitable for all three levels.

The Standard Grade Business Management course covers four areas:

1 What is business?

2 How do businesses develop and perform?

3 What resources do businesses use?

4 How are businesses managed?

There are three assessable elements in the Standard Grade Business Management course. These are:

- Knowledge and Understanding (KU)
- Decision Making (DM)
- Practical Abilities (PA).

The questions in this book cover KU and DM at Foundation, General and Credit Level. Where the questions cover DM, this is indicated by the DM symbol. **DM**

Answers to questions are provided at the back of the book (pages 107–112). Use a jotter or paper for your answers. To answer some questions you will need a calculator, and a ruler for drawing tables.

Practical abilities

- The third assessable element – Practical abilities – is internally assessed.
- It involves the use of a business simulation on a CD-ROM.
- You will complete this as part of your course – it is not a written exam.
- KU and DM skills will be required before you can successfully carry out the CD-ROM tasks.

For example, while using the CD-ROM, you may be required to decide on the location of a business. To do this you will need knowledge about location of industry. This is covered in chapter 3 (pages 46–48).

How to use this book

This revised edition of *Standard Grade Business Management Course Notes* has a clear, easy-to-read layout with a number of features designed to help you understand the course.

Questions

This feature provides you with a range of tasks and activities designed to test your knowledge of the content of the book. This feature also helps as a revision and consolidation activity. Answers to the questions are provided on pages 107–112.

Key terms

Business terms and other words and phrases are defined throughout this book, but those in the key terms feature are of particular importance.

Internet research

This book encourages you to do independent research and mentions a number of websites with useful and interesting information. To find links to these websites, go to: **www.leckieandleckie.co.uk**, click on the Learning Lab button and navigate to the Standard Grade Business Management Course Notes page.

Credit

Material aimed at Credit Level is presented on a coloured background and indicated by the CR symbol.

Case studies

There are several case studies in this book, most of which are real-life features. This will give you information about different types of businesses and industries, as well as give you practice in reading them and answering questions about them. Answers to the case study questions are given on pages 107–112. Case studies are used in the written exam (which tests the KU and DM elements of the course.)

Exam preparation

The questions and case studies in this book will help you to prepare for your Standard Grade Business Management exam. The case studies in this book are longer than the ones in the exam; however, this will stretch you before the exam and can also be used as an introduction to higher work.

- Although it is tempting to look at the answers to questions and case studies first, they will not help you learn much if you do it all the time!
- Learn about each topic, then try the questions, then check the answers.
- Alter your answer as appropriate – do not leave any wrong answer unchanged in case you refer back to it later.

CHAPTER 1
WHAT IS BUSINESS?

What do businesses do?

Goods and services

Businesses produce goods or provide services. Here are some examples:

Goods

- cars
- washing machines
- DVD players
- sweets
- clothes
- seafood

Services

- hairdressing
- car servicing
- insurance
- banking
- education
- public transport
- entertainments (e.g. cinema, theatre)

Tangible Tangible goods are material items which can be seen, touched and handled, such as those listed above in the goods column.

Intangible Services are intangible, which means the services themselves cannot be touched or handled, for example, the service of hairdressing.

Durable Durable goods and services are long-lasting. Goods such as washing machines are durable.

Non-durable Non-durable goods and services are used up quite quickly. Seafood is an example of a non-durable good. Cinema is an example of a non-durable service: it provides entertainment in the form of a film for about 2–3 hours on average. After that, the service is no long available, unless another ticket is purchased.

Consumer goods Consumer goods are sold to people (that is, consumers) for their own use, rather than to other businesses.

Capital goods Capital goods are used by businesses to make consumer goods and other capital goods.

Business types

Sole trader

A sole trader is a business owned and often run by one person, although that person might employ others. Many small businesses such as convenience stores and car mechanics are sole traders.

Partnership

A partnership is a business with between two and twenty partners. Examples include dentists, vets and lawyers. Usually partners enter into a legal agreement which states what share of the profits each partner gets, which partner or partners has most responsibility, and so on. Partners do not always invest the same amount of money, and this can affect their share of the profits.

Private limited company

A private limited company (ltd) is a company whose shares are owned privately. It is owned by the shareholder/s (minimum of one) and run by a board of directors. Such companies are often family businesses.

Public limited company

A public limited company (plc) has shares available for the public to buy on the share market. Requirements for a plc are at least two shareholders and £50,000 share capital. Examples include BP and Arsenal FC.

Hint

Know the main differences between a private limited company and a public limited company. A private limited company does not need to disclose as much information to the public as a public limited company needs to. As a result of this, a private limited company cannot offer shares to the general public or trade on the Stock Exchange. A public limited company can do both of these.

Public ownership

Publicly owned organisations are funded by the taxpayer and are controlled by government. These include public corporations such as the BBC.

Advantages and disadvantages of different types of business

Type of business	*Advantages*	*Disadvantages*
Sole trader	Owner keeps all profits Owner controls all decisions Easy to get business set up	Owner bears all responsibility If owner cannot work, cash flow problems may arise Owner may have difficulty obtaining finance Owner has **unlimited liability**
Partnership	Partners can share workload, according to individual skills A partnership will find it easier than a sole trader to raise finance Risks are shared between partners (e.g. risk of poor profit)	Profits are shared between more people More people running the business increases the chance of disagreement Partners usually have **unlimited liability** A legal agreement needs to be set up
Private limited company	Owners keep control of the business A private limited company can raise more finance than a smaller business Shareholders have **limited liability**	Profits are shared among more people A legal agreement must be set up Shares cannot be sold to public, so raising finance is harder than for a public limited company
Public limited company	A plc can raise more finance and borrow more money Shareholders have **limited liability**	A plc has no control over who buys shares High costs of setting up the company Accounts must be published annually
Public ownership	Less competition	May not be as profitable as private sector businesses

Unlimited liability A sole trader, or people in an unlimited partnership, have full responsibility (or liability) for the debts of their firm. This means that if the firm does not have enough funds to pay off debts, then the owner or partners must pay off the debts from their personal funds and assets. This can lead to them losing their home, car and other assets.

Limited liability In a limited liability company, shareholders (in a limited company or a plc) or partners (in a limited liability partnership) are only liable for the amount they invested in the firm. For example, if a firm does not have enough funds to pay off its debts, a shareholder who invested £100 could lose that amount. However, the shareholder will not have to pay off the firm's debts from their own assets.

Internet research

Although partners often have unlimited liability, people can form limited partnerships and limited liability partnerships in business. Look for more information by searching the term 'limited partnership' on the Wikipedia website.

Links to this site and other websites relating to Standard Grade Business Management can be found at: **www.leckieandleckie.co.uk** by clicking on the Learning Lab button and navigating to the Standard Grade Business Management Course Notes page.

Business sizes

Small businesses

Usual features:

- owned (and often run) by one person, that is, a sole trader OR
- owned and run by between two and twenty people, that is, a partnership
- tend to sell goods and services locally
- employ fewer than 50 people.

Medium-sized businesses

Usual features:

- owned and run by a group of people (e.g. partners, shareholders or directors)
- can sell goods and services locally and/or nationally
- employ between 50 and 250 people.

Large businesses

Usual features:

- owned by a large number of people (shareholders) and run by people appointed by them (directors)
- produce and/or sell goods and services in several locations – often in several countries
- employ more than 250 people – sometimes hundreds of thousands.

Charities

Charities are organisations which aim to care for those in need of help, using donations from the public. They also raise funds in other ways. They do not aim to make a profit. Examples include Oxfam, RSPCA and Save the Children.

Sectors of the economy

Private, public and voluntary sectors

The three sectors of the economy are defined by **ownership** (private or public money) and **motive** (profit-making or non-profit-making).

Private

- Sole traders, partnerships, limited companies, public limited companies
- Owned by sole trader, partners, shareholders
- Private money from shareholders, bank loans

Public

- Nationalised industries, local authority services, schools and hospitals
- Owned by the state
- Public money from taxes

Voluntary

- Charities, youth clubs, golf clubs
- Administered by officials
- Money from donations and gifts

Sectors of industry

Primary, secondary and tertiary sectors

The three divisions are defined by the **type of product or service produced**, that is, raw materials (primary sector), manufactured goods (secondary sector) or services (tertiary sector).

Primary (extractive)	*Secondary (manufacturing)*	*Tertiary (service)*
Oil production	Car manufacturing	Insurance
Fishing	Engineering industry	Hairdressing
Forestry	Shipbuilding	Leisure industry
	Wine production	Public transport
		Fire service
		Education

CASE STUDY: FISHING INDUSTRY IN SCOTLAND

Fishing is an important environmental and economic issue for Scotland. If too many fish are caught, there may not be enough fish in future. If limits on catches are too low, some Scottish fishermen may lose their livelihood

Scotland is among the largest **sea fishing** nations in Europe. It accounts for 66% of landings in the UK. Fishing occurs mainly in the North Sea, the west of Scotland and around the Faroe Islands. Catches include cod, plaice and langoustine.

Fish farming began in Scotland in the 1970s. Fish are cultivated and kept in water enclosures or tanks. Today the industry employs about 2000 people directly and 4000–5000 in supporting sectors. Most (75%) of the jobs are in the Highlands and Islands. The industry accounts for around 50% in monetary terms of all Scottish food exports. Products include salmon, rainbow trout and cultivated shellfish.

Questions on case study

1 **a** What sector of industry does fishing come into?

b Why does it come into this sector?

2 State one difference and one similarity between sea fishing and fish farming.

3 Copy out the table shown below, and complete it from information in the case study.

Examples of fish produced in Scotland	
Sea (wild) fish	Farmed fish

4 How important is fish farming to the Scottish food exporting industry and to the economy of the Highlands and Islands? Explain your answer.

Internet research

Visit the Scottish Executive website. From the Fisheries section write some notes on the environmental effects that can occur if farmed fish escape.

Links to this site and other websites relating to Standard Grade Business Management can be found at: **www.leckieandleckie.co.uk** by clicking on the Learning Lab button and navigating to the Standard Grade Business Management Course Notes page.

Needs and wants

CR

Needs

These are what people must have in order to survive, that is, basic needs.

Wants

After basic needs are met, people often wish for more. These desires are called wants and are unlimited. They include needs and also cover items people would like to have just because they are available. These items give the consumer satisfaction.

Production and consumption

In the production of goods, several businesses might be involved. The production of cream cakes, for example, could include the following processes:

The farmer produces wheat | *The miller produces flour* | *The baker produces the cakes and adds the cream* | *The retailer sells the cake to Mrs White* | *Mrs White's son consumes (eats) the cake*

- **Production** is the process of making goods so that they can either be consumed, or go on to another stage of production as shown above. North Sea oil cannot be used until it is extracted from under the sea. Fish cannot be eaten until they go through several stages of production – these include catching the fish, gutting them, and making them available to consumers at market stalls and retailers.
- **Consumption** involves the purchasing of goods and services. In many cases it also involves using them up, e.g. services and non-durable (short-life) goods such as fresh food.

Creating wealth

Wealth creation occurs at each stage of the production process described above. Value is added by each producer (farmer, miller, baker, retailer) so that the total value of the cream cakes will be much more than the total value of the wheat, cream and sugar, that is, the raw materials used. Therefore each stage creates more total wealth than the previous stage.

Questions 1

1 **a** Name one difference between the private and public sectors of the economy.

b What is the difference between needs and wants?

CR

c What is meant by the following terms:

(i) production

(ii) consumption

2 **a** What is the term for a business owned by one person?

b What is the usual maximum number of partners in a partnership?

c Small businesses usually employ fewer than ___ people. What is the missing figure?

d Name two differences between small and large businesses.

e What type of organisation is described below?

'Its main aim is to care for those in need of help using donations from the public and funds raised in other ways. It does not aim to make a profit.'

3 **a** Name three different types of businesses and/or producers which might be involved from the raw material stage to the final production of an oak table.

b The table is put up for sale in a large furniture store which is owned by shareholders and aims to maximise profit. The store employs 50–250 people.

(i) The store belongs to a sector of the economy and a sector of industry. Choose the correct one from each list:

Economy: private, public, voluntary

Industry: primary, secondary, tertiary

(ii) Is the store an example of a small, medium or large business? Give a reason for your answer.

c Write a paragraph explaining what is meant by the term 'creating wealth'.

d State how wealth might be created between each of the processes which you named in part **a**.

Why do businesses exist?

Reasons for the existence of businesses

Four of the different reasons for the existence of businesses are:

- enterprise
- profit
- charity
- public service.

Enterprise

to develop a new idea, that is, to show enterprise (see also page 21)

Profit

to make a profit, that is, to earn more money than is spent: sales less costs

Charity

for charitable reasons, e.g. raising funds to give to victims of earthquakes

Public service

to provide public services such as the NHS, schools and hospitals

Entrepreneurship

An **entrepreneur** is someone who has an idea for a business venture, or is prepared to take another person's idea and develop it. The entrepreneur is prepared to finance it (or encourage other people to do so) and, taking a risk, will turn it into a new product or service. This willingness to push forward and take risks is called **enterprise**.

Linda Bennett (LK Bennett) and Richard Branson (the Virgin Group) are two examples of entrepreneurs. Other examples of entrepreneurs are seen in the TV programme 'The Dragons' Den'. The millionaires who offer to invest money are entrepreneurs, as are the people who show them their ideas.

An entrepreneur needs the following skills and qualities:

- is creative and energetic
- has enthusiasm for the task
- will use their own initiative
- will take risks
- is assertive
- is a decision maker
- can handle different aspects of business
- is a problem solver.

The first few years of a new business are particularly risky.

Risks faced by new businesses

Risks include:

- people not buying the product or service
- profits might not be high enough to cover costs in the long term
- cash flow may not cover day-to-day expenses
- more money may be owed than can be paid back in the long term
- all the money which was invested may be lost.

For more on risks faced by new businesses, see page 22.

Aims of organisations and businesses

Private sector aims

- To make a profit
- To provide goods/services
- To increase market share
- To survive
- To grow
- To make customers happy
- To develop employees

Voluntary sector aims

- To raise funds for good causes
- To raise awareness of their cause
- To inform and educate the public
- To provide a service

Public sector aims

- To provide public goods/services
- To make customers happy
- To cover costs or break-even
- To develop employees

Costs and benefits of business

Social benefits and costs

Social benefits are positive things which happen to a community as a result of local businesses. Examples include better roads, improved housing and new schools.

Social costs are the negative effects on a community caused by some local businesses. Examples include air/ noise/ water pollution, heavy traffic, health problems, or inconvenience arising from building work and redevelopment.

Economic benefits and costs

Economic benefits and costs usually involve finance in some way. **Economic benefits** are the positive monetary effects local businesses have on a community. An example is increased income for local people as a result of local jobs. This in turn leads to increased spending in the area which helps other local businesses. Both of these factors help to raise the standard of living in an area.

Examples of **economic costs** are increased community taxes on property, and increased expenditure on infrastructure.

CASE STUDY: ANTONINE CENTRE

A new phase of Cumbernauld Town Centre, called the Antonine Centre, was opened in June 2007.

The opening of the £45 million mall is a huge boost to the local retail sector and to the local economy. A jobs fair attracted 1600 locals who were interested in applying for the 300 vacancies within the centre. Specially tailored training courses were offered to 37 unemployed individuals to prepare them for careers in retail. Well known names such as Next and Dunns, and the nearby Tesco store are expected to boost trade at Cumbernauld Town Centre.

However, the redevelopment has not pleased everyone. Some shops in the older parts of the town centre were adversely affected during the building work. A car park was closed while work started on the new phase, and customers had to enter from the other side of the building, which put some customers off. One resident complained that there is no longer ramp access for baby buggies to the older parts of the town centre.

It is hoped, however, that the new centre will give the people of Cumbernauld the choice of shopping that people from similar size towns enjoy, and that shops in the older parts will benefit from the rise in customers brought in by the Antonine Centre.

Questions on case study

1 As a result of the new Antonine Centre, name and describe one economic benefit to:
   - **a** businesses in Cumbernauld's town centre
   - **b** local people in Cumbernauld.

2 One resident had difficulty entering the old town centre with her child's buggy. What kind of cost does this represent?

3 State two ways in which you think the new Antonine Centre might help raise the standard of living in Cumbernauld.

4 What economic costs did some retailers face during the development of the Antonine Centre?

Stakeholders

Stakeholders are people with any interest in or an influence on an organisation. They can include people who have no financial interest in it such as environmental groups, and those who do have financial interest such as shareholders and employees. (For more on stakeholders, see page 44.)

Stakeholders of a large football club which is a public limited company (plc)

- *shareholders*
- *media*
- *directors*

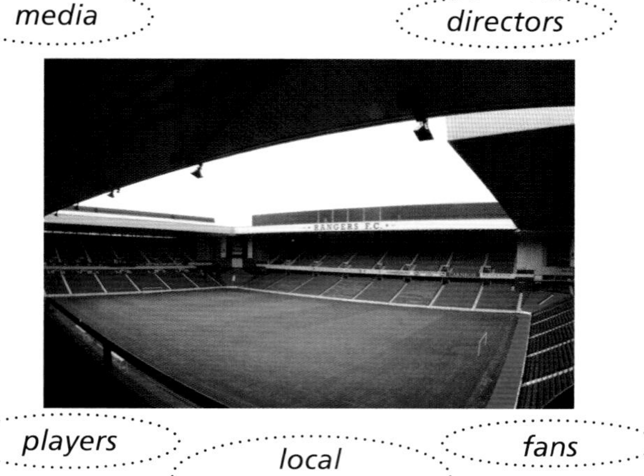

- *players*
- *local residents*
- *fans*

Stakeholders of a manufacturing plc

- *shareholders*
- *suppliers*
- *inland revenue*
- *customers*
- *directors*
- *employees*

Interests of stakeholders in a football club

This example illustrates a large club, which is a plc:

Stakeholders	Possible interests	Possible influences
Shareholders	To receive a share of profits made and to see their club make progress in the appropriate leagues and win games.	To maximise profits (and therefore dividends) shareholders might encourage higher ticket prices and lower running costs. They can vote at the annual general meeting where shareholders and directors meet.
Players	To win games and build an excellent reputation for their club. They then increase their own chances of an increased income, good reputation, sponsorship deals, etc.	A top class player can bring in sponsorship deals and publicity for the club.
Directors	To ensure the long-term success of the club; to make healthy profits as they might also be shareholders.	Directors influence the direction that a club takes. Directors need to balance the need to make profits (enabling to club to survive, if not grow and become increasingly successful) with the needs of fans (e.g. affordable season's tickets).
Media	If the public want to find out about their favourite stars, they watch or listen to the media who will give that information. It is in the interest of the media to do this. Viewers and listeners mean money, which is usually raised from advertising revenue.	The media can influence the popularity of a sport, for example, darts became much more of a profit making activity when it was televised. The media also helps sports like football to make money because they have to pay leagues and clubs for the privilege of televising matches. Media coverage of certain stories can also affect outcomes.
Local residents	They may suffer the social costs of a large stadium nearby when games are on. This could include bad behaviour from passing fans and large crowds passing by on their way to games. They may also benefit from increased trade in pubs and shops on match days, and from community sports projects run by the club.	Local residents will want disruption to their local area minimised, so may complain to authorities, or may not attend matches if unhappy.
Fans	They are interested in attending or watching matches. They have an interest in the state of the grounds, the skill of the players, the efficiency of the manager and directors. Many will also be shareholders.	Many clubs have fans associations through which they can discuss, and influence, the running of their clubs.

Hint

Make sure you know the difference between shareholders and stakeholders. Shareholders are financial investors in a business; stakeholders are anyone with an interest in or an influence on a company and can include shareholders.

Questions 2

1 a To start up a business requires 'enterprise'. What is meant by this term?

b What is the name given to someone who has 'enterprise'? Name two real-life examples of this type of person.

c Business can be divided into the private sector, public sector or voluntary sector.

(i) Marks & Spencer is in the private sector. Give another example of a private sector organisation.

(ii) Name one organisation in each of the other two sectors, that is, public and voluntary.

(iii) Each of the organisations you named in parts (i) and (ii) have different aims. State what you think the main aim of each one of the three organisations is likely to be.

(iv) Give examples of two stakeholders in each organisation named in parts (i) and (ii). In each case, state what their main interest in the organisation might be.

d Name three risks which a person starting a new business might face during the first year of business.

2 The Blue Sox Football Club plc is a large, profit-making organisation. Copy and complete the table below, listing three stakeholders and their possible interests and influence in the club. An example is given to help you.

Stakeholders	*Possible interest/influence*
Fans	Attending/watching matches. Some will also be shareholders who are interested in the profits too.

3 Businesses can bring social costs and benefits to their local communities. They can also bring economic costs and benefits.

a What is the difference between social costs and social benefits? Give two examples of each.

b What is the difference between economic costs and economic benefits? Give two examples of each.

How are businesses organised?

Organisation structures

The structure of an organisation can be shown as a chart. An example is shown at the top of page 17.

Line relationships

Line relationships refer to links between bosses and people who work for them. In a chart like the one shown on page 17, these lines tend to be vertical (that is, up and down).

Organisation chart of Brightspark Department Store

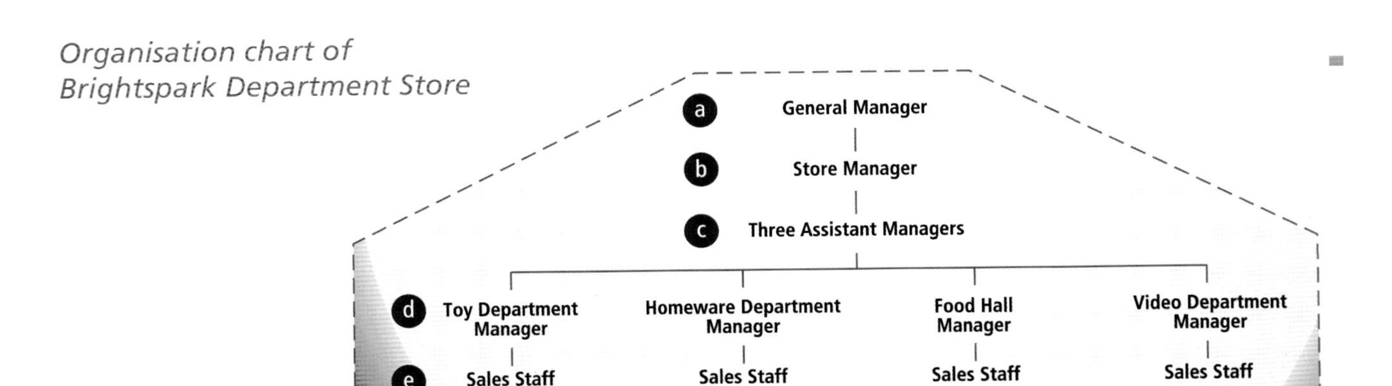

- a The organisation chart shows who is in charge – the general manager.
- b The next in charge, and directly responsible to the general manager is the store manager. There is a line relationship between the two. The general manager is the line manager to the store manager.
- c The three assistant managers come next in line of authority and are directly responsible to the store manager and indirectly to the general manager. The store manager is their line manager.
- d The four departmental managers are below the assistant managers in authority. The three assistant managers collectively have authority over the four departmental managers.
- e The sales staff in each department are directly responsible to the appropriate departmental manager. There is a direct line relationship between them.

Lateral relationships

Lateral relationships are between people at the same level. In the above chart, the toy department manager and the homeware department manager are on the same level of authority, and this is shown by a horizontal line, also known as **lateral**.

Brightspark Department Store has four levels of management: the general manager, the store manager, the assistant managers, and the departmental managers. However, the organisation of Brown and Black Ltd has only two levels of management: the manager and the assistant manager.

Organisation chart of Brown and Black Ltd

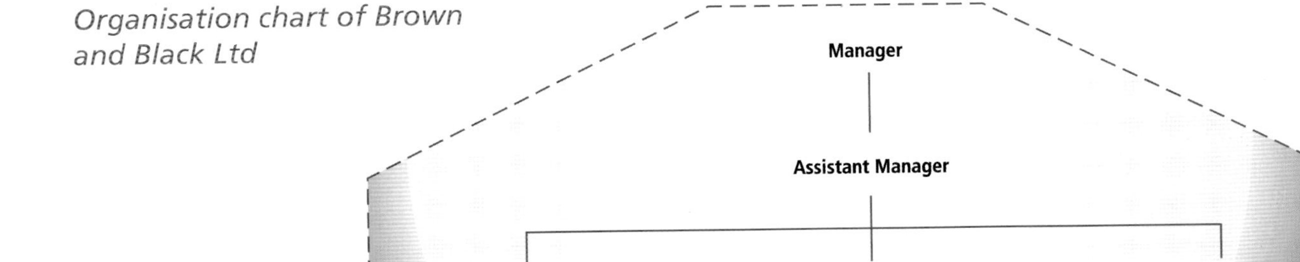

Brown and Black Ltd, therefore, has a flatter structure than Brightspark Department Store: there are fewer managers. This can be shown in another way, as shown on page 18.

Tall and flat structures

In Brightspark Department Store, the line of communications upwards is sales staff, department manager, assistant managers, store manager, general manager, and back the same way. This is called the **chain of command**.

In Brown and Black Ltd the line of communication is salesperson, assistant manager, manager. Communication should go back through the same lines (again, the chain of command). There are fewer levels to go through in Brown and Black Ltd, so communication and decision making is quicker. There are fewer levels of responsibility and authority in a flat structure, so employees can show more initiative and are more motivated.

A tall structure

Brightspark Department Store, with many levels of management, is an example of a tall structure.

A flat structure

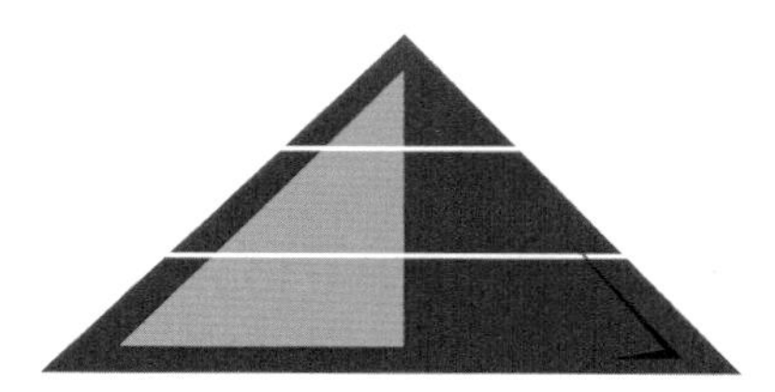

Brown and Black Ltd, with fewer levels of management, is an example of a flat structure.

Newer organisations tend to have flatter structures whether they are large or small. The tall structure is a more traditional approach, used by the Armed Forces and the Civil Service for example.

Span of control

CR

In tall structures, there is usually a narrow span of control. In flat structures, the span of control is likely to be wide. This can be shown diagrammatically.

When there is a wide span of control, those in authority supervise a greater number of people. For example, Mrs B has direct authority over six people, and Mr C has direct authority over five people.

When there is a narrow span of control, each manager or director has authority over fewer people. Mr A has direct authority over two people, as do both Ms X and Mrs M.

In the example showing a wide span of control, each manager has direct authority over more people than any of the managers in the narrow span of control.

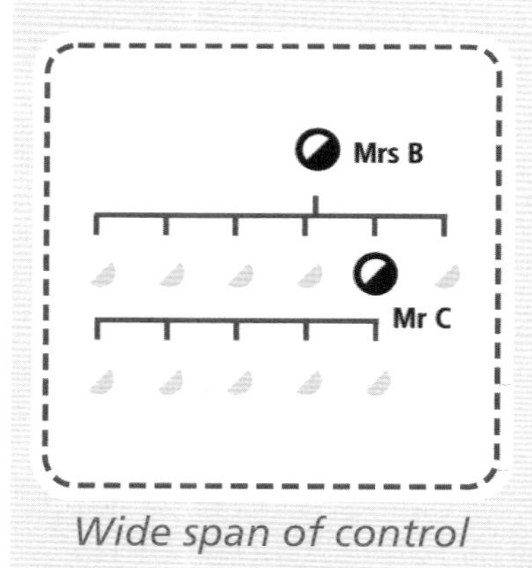

Wide span of control

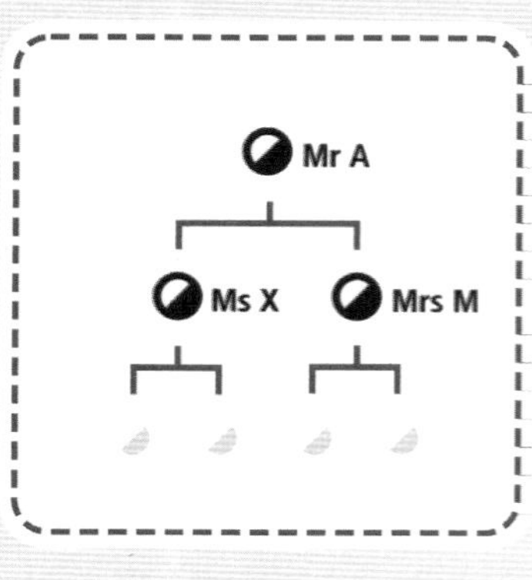

Narrow span of control

Functional areas of business

There are four **functional areas** of business. These are:

- **marketing** – including market research and development, advertising and promotion
- **human resources** – including recruitment, training, industrial relations, management styles and organisation
- **operations** – designing, producing and distributing goods
- **finance** – including raising finance, budgeting, cash flow, final accounts and ratios and their analysis.

In addition, administration and ICT (Information and Communication Technology) offer support to the whole business. For example, the ICT section is responsible for maintaining computer systems throughout the business – purchasing hardware and software, training staff, establishing procedures, and maintaining appropriate security systems. Administration provides a range of services to support other functional areas, including reception duties, handling customer service enquiries, record keeping and file management, word processing services and general support duties.

These **functional areas** are completely distinct from **functional relationships**.

Functional relationships

CR

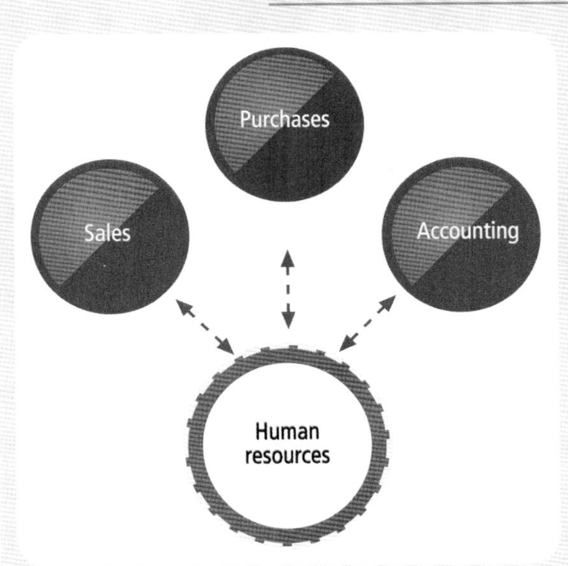

When one department offers direct services to other departments it is said to have a **functional relationship** with these departments. However, all areas of a business should relate to each other, and depend on each other, and therefore they too have functional relationships.

Marketing promotes the work of other areas such as operations, helping to sell products and services by making the public aware of them and their features (through advertising).

Human resources has a functional relationship with the other areas because it recruits and looks after the welfare and records of all staff in these departments.

The operations part of a business could be seen as the hub of the business in that it includes design, production and distribution. However, without marketing, and finance, goods are less likely to be sold. On the other hand, marketing and finance on their own are of no use unless there is something to sell!

The area of finance provides funds for departments so that they can function and the whole organisation keep going. It gets this money from buyers of the goods and services the organisation sells.

Administration also offers services to other areas, so it too has a functional relationship with them. In a factory producing canned drinks, administration will deal with phone calls, meetings and ICT-based support such as word-processing.

Responsibility Having responsibility means being answerable for actions and decisions taken by oneself and/or others.

Authority Having authority means having the power/right to take a certain action and to delegate to others. It also includes responsibility. People with authority will always have the responsibility that authority brings. Most people have some responsibility for their actions and decisions. This does not mean that they have authority, however. Responsibility does not automatically bring authority, but authority does (or should!) bring responsibility.

Questions 3

1 a The diagrams below demonstrate two organisation structures. What are they called?

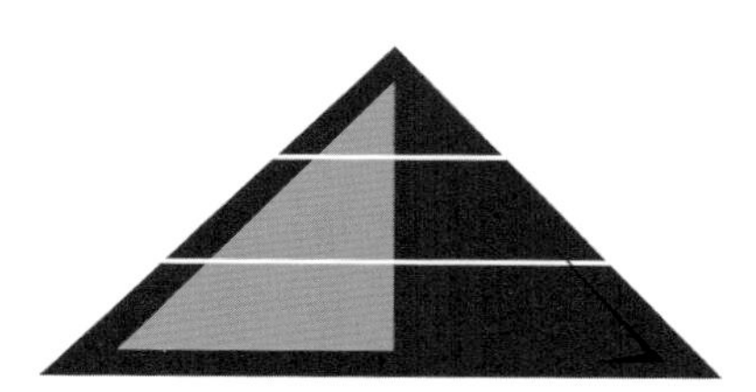

b (i) What are the main differences between the two structures?

(ii) Which one represents a more traditional approach to business organisation?

c Draw a simple diagram to illustrate line relationships, and state what they mean.

d What is meant by the term 'span of control'? Use diagrams to illustrate your answer.

e Administration and Human resources have 'functional relationships' with other areas in an organisation.

(i) What is a 'functional relationship'?

(ii) Name two services which:

A Administration gives to other areas

B Human resources gives to other areas.

f Showing clearly the difference between the two, give a definition of both:

(i) authority

(ii) responsibility

CHAPTER 2
HOW DO BUSINESSES DEVELOP AND PERFORM?

How do businesses start?

Enterprise

The concept of enterprise is illustrated in the following diagram:

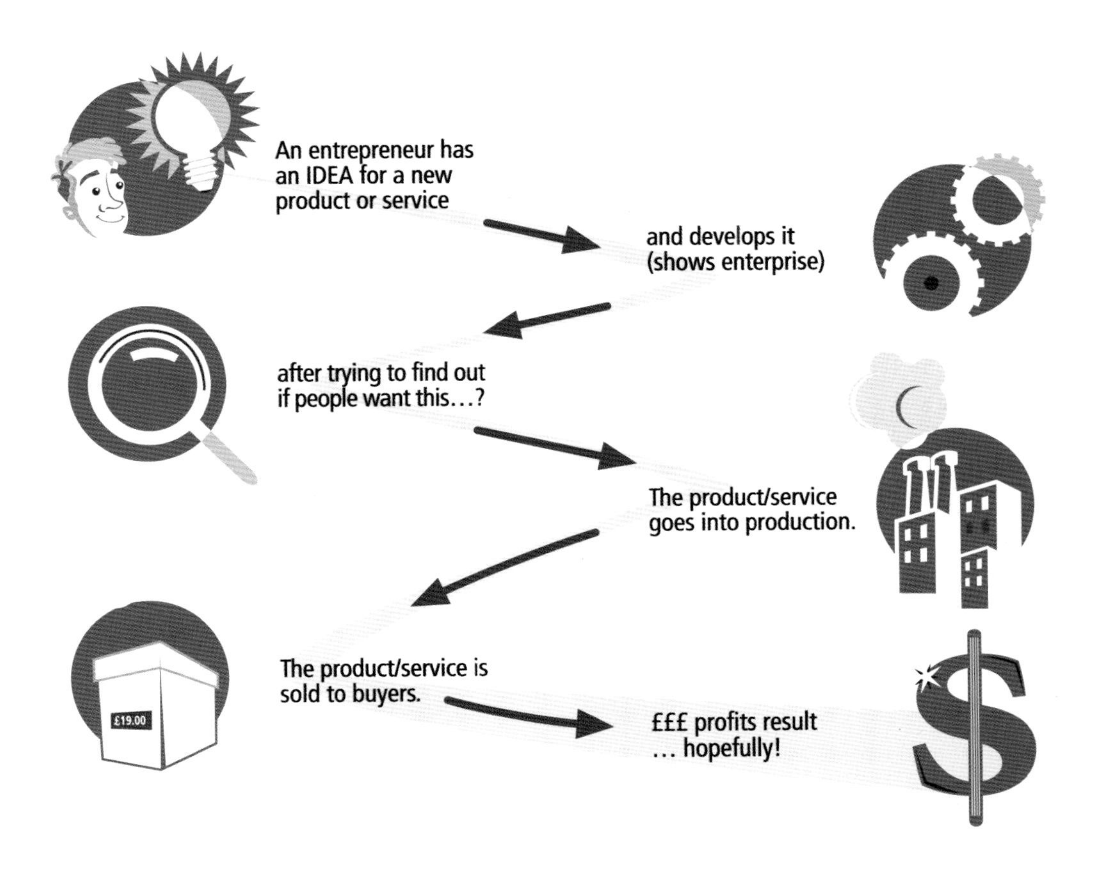

External information and advice

The entrepreneur may need help before reaching the profit-making stage. This help can be in the form of finance or advice.

Finance

- loan or overdraft from banks or other financial institutions
- grant from government or other source, e.g. the Prince's Trust
- loan from family and friends
- finance from partners
- credit from suppliers (i.e. buy now, pay later)

Advice

- government agencies/local authorities
- development agencies
- business partners and/or friends
- consultants

Hint

For more information on finance and advice, see pages 48–51.

Identifying risk

Entrepreneurs take the risks of:

- no-one buying the product or service
- losing all the money invested
- not being able to pay expenses
- losing personal assets (e.g. their house or car).

There are always risks in business. If these risks are carefully considered and planned for, business shouldn't be a gamble. Three examples of identifying and planning for risks are:

- **budgeting for expenses**

  Careful budgeting and planning is essential to make sure that all expenses can be paid. Costs can be budgeted for to ensure that loans and savings are high enough to cope with expected expenditure. There should also be a reserve for unexpected expenditure.
- **the break-even point should be calculated**

  The break-even point is the point at which costs/expenses and income are equal, that is, there is no net loss or gain.
- **keeping reserves of cash**

  If possible, reserves of cash should be kept for emergencies, to avoid the risk of losing all the money invested.

Careful market research should be done to make sure that:

- there is demand for the product
- the correct price is set for the product.

If planning is carefully done, risks are greatly reduced. Careful planning (in advance) and monitoring (day-to-day checking) are vital. See page 13 for more information about risk.

Internet research

Visit the Prince's Scottish Youth Business Trust. List the help that the Trust offers to entrepreneurs aged 18–25 if they want to start their own business.

Links to this site and other websites relating to Standard Grade Business Management can be found at: **www.leckieandleckie.co.uk** by clicking on the Learning Lab button and navigating to the Standard Grade Business Management Course Notes page.

LECKIE&LECKIE Learning Lab

The market

All businesses require a **market** – a way of selling their goods or services.

A market can be a place where buyers and sellers physically meet, as in the following examples:

- outdoor market
- shopping mall
- high street shop
- ice-cream van.

However, other markets include:

- mail order
- dispensing machine (e.g. dispensing cash, sweets or soft drinks)
- door-to-door delivery (e.g. Betterware, Avon)
- telephone sales (e.g. double-glazing)
- TV shopping channels
- internet
- the housing market.

Market If people buy the products and/or services in sufficient quantity, there is said to be a market for them. The two vital components of a market are buyers and sellers.

Researching the market

Entrepreneurs try to cut down the risks that consumers:

- don't want the product or service
- like the product or service but don't like the price
- find it difficult to locate the product or service.

To reduce such risks, entrepreneurs should research the market before starting full production.

Market segments

The market – customers – can be grouped or sorted using a range of criteria. This is called **market segmentation**, and it is a useful tool in market research because it helps businesses target specific groups better. The market may be divided by:

- age
- gender
- religion
- ethnicity
- occupation or income
- socio-economic group or 'class'
- location.

Researching the market – new and existing products

Field research

Field research involves obtaining first-hand information, i.e. **primary data**. It is where people's opinions are directly sought. The information from this field research can be gained by:

- observing consumers' responses to a product, e.g. watching children's reactions to a prototype toy
- using surveys and/or questionnaires where people's written opinions about a product are sought
- using consumer panels or focus groups to discuss a product and listen to opinions
- testing the market – choosing a smaller, limited area (e.g. the north of England) in which to pilot or sell products before selling them to the UK as a whole.

Advantages of field research	*Disadvantages of field research*
Data is collected for a specific purpose so it is more likely to be relevant and accurate	Information gathered has to be analysed which is time consuming (and possibly) expensive
Large audiences can be targeted for some of the methods used, e.g. telephone surveys	If interviews are used, interviewers have to be trained, which can be costly
If interviews are used, the interviewer can clarify questions	
Some methods such as telephone and postal surveys can be relatively inexpensive	

Desk research

This involves studying and evaluating **secondary data**. This is information which already exists in easy-to-access form (it will have originally been gathered for another purpose). This information can be from the internet, CD-ROMs, news media, journals and books.

Advantages of desk research	*Disadvantages of desk research*
Easy to find because it is already in existence	Since the data was collected for one purpose, it might not be totally accurate, or relevant, for another
More cost effective because it does not have to be collected by interviewers, nor do surveys have to be compiled	It may be difficult to identify and extract relevant information from existing research

Effectiveness of market research

The effectiveness of market research will depend on a number of factors:

- the accuracy of the information received
- the money available to spend on the research
- targeting the correct segments of the market and/or the correct secondary data
- making the right conclusions.

Sometimes a company will pilot a new product even after
out extensive market research. An example of such pilotin
product is sold in only one region of the country. If the pro
as the research suggested (that is, confirming the market r
product would be sold nationally, then perhaps internation

Creating a prototype

It is too expensive to go into full production of a new produ
producer is absolutely sure that the product is suitable and that there is a market for it. So, before launching a new product, a **prototype** (a working model or example) is often made. The producer can use the prototype to demonstrate features of the new product to potential consumers to find out their opinion of the item. Changes will probably be made to the product as a result of such feedback. Potential customers will probably also be asked for their opinions on suitable prices, packaging and sales outlets.

Resources

Resources come into four main categories (known as **factors of production**):

- **Land** – natural resources (including water, trees, fields and the things produced from them such as oil, fish, fruit, vegetables).
- **Labour** – human workers of all kinds.
- **Capital** – includes money, buildings and machinery.
- **Enterprise** – the development of ideas, and the drive to put them into action. Enterprise uses Land, Labour and Capital to get an organisation started and moving forward.

Business plan

A business plan outlines the objectives of a business and how it intends to achieve these objectives. Business plans differ from business to business, but in general they cover the following areas.

- **General details about the business**
  - name
  - objectives (what it hopes to achieve)
  - proposed location
  - type of ownership (e.g. sole trader, partnership or limited company)
- **Human resources**
  - key people in the business
  - required skills
  - positions of authority and responsibility
  - wages and salaries
- **The product or service**
  - nature of product or service to be produced or provided
  - quantity to be produced or provided
  - price of the product or service
  - market research required

- **The market**
  - market to be targeted (e.g. by age, sex, income, occupation)
  - size and potential growth of the market
  - results of market research
  - intentions about advertising and promotion
- **Premises and equipment**
  - location of premises
  - cost of premises and equipment
  - type of premises and equipment
  - amount of equipment required
  - expected lifespan, e.g. 10-year lease
- **Profit estimates**
  - forecast of sales
  - costs and break-even points
  - projected timescale for profit-making
- **Cash flow**
  - cash budgets for future period
  - expected income and expenditure
  - source(s) of income
  - scale of loan or overdraft needed
- **Capital**
  - source of initial funding (i.e. all from the owner(s) or partially from loan)

A business plan is usually shown to an external agency such as a bank. If the bank is going to lend money to the business, it will want to see clear plans of the business's intentions.

Questions 1

Picture A
Nasim Mawji—Entrepreneur

Picture B
Group of teenagers

1. **a** Which picture shows the buyers and which one shows the sellers?
   b Name two risks which Nasim Mawji may have faced when starting her business.
   c Help is available for entrepreneurs. List two sources of financial help which might have been available to Nasim.
   d List two sources of general advice which Nasim might find useful.
2. **a** What are the two vital components of a market?
   b Name four types of market where the two components mentioned in part **a** physically meet.

c Draw a two-column table.
(i) In the first column, list the four factors of production.
(ii) In the second column, list two examples of each one.

3 Before a business starts up, it is expected that the owners will know something about the market for their product or service.
a Name the two main ways of researching the market.
b Define each term given in your answer to part **a**. Show clearly the difference between them, giving examples of each.
c Name two ways of avoiding some of the risks which a new business faces.

4 a Write a brief description of a business plan.
b (i) Name one important external agency which is likely to see this plan.
(ii) What is the likely purpose of showing the business plan to this agency?
c Name and describe five main areas covered by a good business plan.

How do businesses grow?

A successful product or service can lead to **expansion**. This expansion may be internal, external, or a combination of the two.

Internal expansion

Internal expansion means expansion (growth) of an existing business within itself.

Here is a simple example of internal expansion:

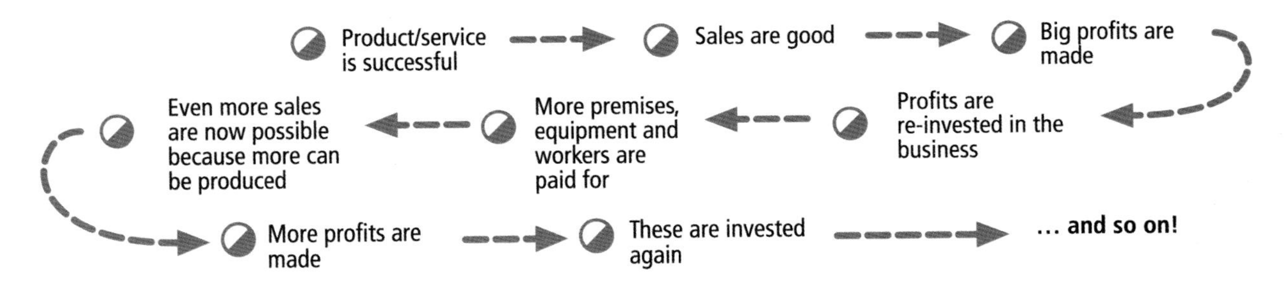

External expansion

External expansion means expansion of a business through outside influences. These include:

merger or amalgamation

Two or more businesses (usually of a similar size) agree to join together to create one business.

takeover (acquisition)

In a takeover one business buys another. Usually the one making the takeover is the larger one.

Combination of internal and external expansion

Some businesses grow by a combination of internal and external expansion. A small business may grow internally at first, and then be taken over by, or merge with, another company later.

Integration

Integration involves the creation of one business out of two or more previously separate businesses. Mergers, amalgamations and takeovers are examples of integration.

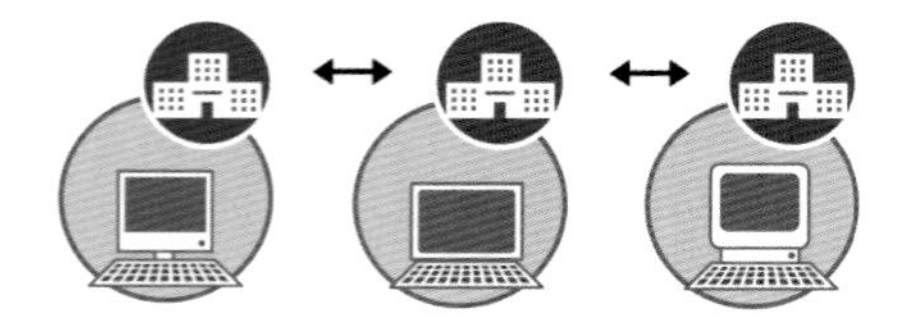

Horizontal integration

This illustration shows an example of horizontal integration. Each business produces the same or similar product, and is at the same stage of production.

Forward vertical integration

These businesses are in the same industry, but at different stages of production.

The organisation at the beginning of the chain, i.e. the owners of the forest, take over the factory, which in turn takes over the store.

This is called forward vertical integration because the takeover starts from the beginning of the chain, and it involves different stages of production being taken over, unlike the horizontal integration example above.

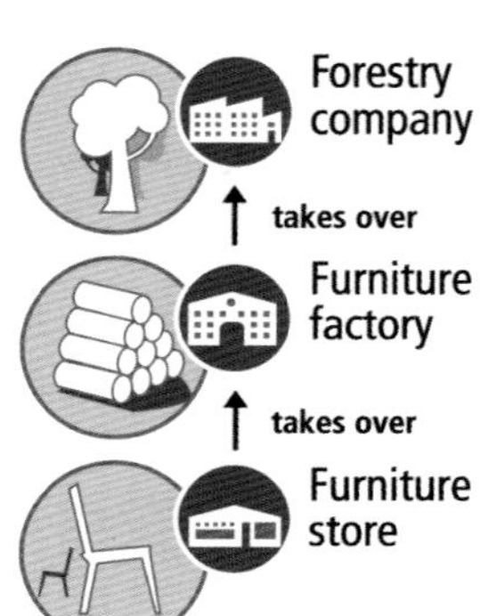

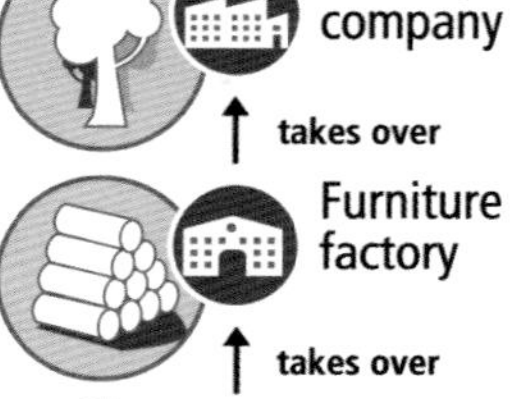

Backward vertical integration

Backward vertical integration is when the last business in the chain, i.e. the furniture store, takes over the stage before it, i.e. the factory, which in turn takes over the first stage of production, i.e. the forest.

Diversification

- Some businesses diversify into completely different products.
- These businesses are known as **conglomerates**.
- This can safeguard the business.
- Businesses can diversify by merging with, or taking over, other businesses.
- They can also diversify by going into the production of other products and services by themselves (internal diversification).

The company shown here produces very different products and services. If the CD division stops making profits and collapses, there are three other ranges of goods and services which may help the company to survive.

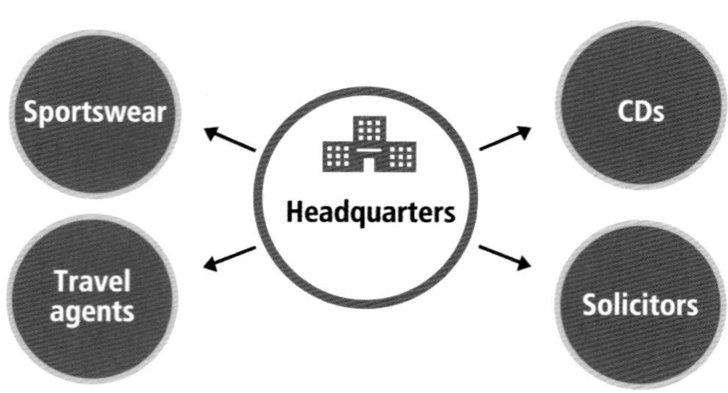

Internet research

Visit the Business Link website. Use the search tool to find the section on mergers. Take some notes on the benefits and pitfalls of mergers.

Unilever is an example of a company that has diversified. Visit the Unilever website, and make a note of at least six different product types that the company makes.

Links to these sites and other websites relating to Standard Grade Business Management can be found at: **www.leckieandleckie.co.uk** by clicking on the Learning Lab button and navigating to the Standard Grade Business Management Course Notes page.

Innovation

- Innovation means developing new ideas and making discoveries.
- It can also involve creating new solutions for old problems.
- For innovations to be of any commercial use a company must also be prepared to implement them.

Businesses operate in a competitive environment. In order to grow, businesses must keep ahead of, or at least up to date with, competitors. This means being aware of new inventions, discoveries and procedures of others too.

Research and development

CR

In order to grow in size, or stay competitive, companies often have to carry out research and development on new products and services to see if they are **viable**. They then carry out market research to see if there is a market for the product or service.

CASE STUDY: ALTON TOWERS – THE OBLIVION RIDE

The Oblivion Ride at Alton Towers theme park opened in March 1998 and is still operating today.

Since the cost of production and operation was going to be high, the organisation had to be sure it was going in the right direction with the development of the product. It had to ask the following questions:

- Will people want to go on the new rollercoaster?
- What kind of rollercoaster should it be?

Research

The organisation had to carry out two main types of research before spending a lot of money – market research and product research. Research costs money but not nearly as much as building a new rollercoaster which no-one wants to go on!

Market research

Firstly the organisation had to identify the market, that is, what type of people would be interested in a new rollercoaster (e.g. young, old, male, female). The organisation then investigated whether a new rollercoaster would appeal to that market, and if so, what kind of rollercoaster.

Answers to questions like 'Would you like a new rollercoaster in the theme park, and if so why?' were important, as were indications of what people would like a rollercoaster ride to contain, and how much they would pay.

Once it was established that there was a demand for it, the next stage was product research.

Product research

This involved experiments with materials, size of the product and prototypes. The business drew plans of the new rollercoaster and budgeted the costs of bringing these plans to life. It researched the materials needed and the engineering calculations which were required. The location was also very important.

Development

The new product needed to be developed:

- a scale model was built
- the site was chosen and cleared
- building began
- the operation and safety of the rollercoaster were tested many times
- a name was chosen for the rollercoaster
- advertising and promotion took place.

Questions on case study

1. Give two reasons why it was so important to carry out market and product research before fully developing the Oblivion ride.
2. The product was then developed. Why do you think that safety testing was so important in its development?
3. Name two other things that were carried out during the development stage of the product.

Market led When a firm does research to find out what consumers want, it is said to be **market led** in its approach.

Product led When a company produces what it thinks will work with little or no market research, this is known as a **product-led** approach.

Reasons for growth

A business will decide to grow for a number of reasons:

- to increase profit
- to gain market control – creating a larger business which may then have the majority share of the market
- to control raw materials – to ensure that the business receives the appropriate supplies on time
- to achieve economies of scale (see below)
- to diversify (see page 28)
- to remove competitors from the market, e.g. by taking them over.

Economies of scale

Economies of scale These are the financial benefits that an organisation gains when it grows bigger. These include examples such as cheaper costs per unit to produce goods and cheaper costs per unit to transport goods.

Internal economies of scale come from within the business; external economies come from or affect the world outside the business. In contrast, diseconomies of scale occur when unit costs increase as the business gets bigger.

Internal economies

- **Technical economies** – large businesses can afford automation, computerisation and technology. These often produce more goods in a given time. As a result, the unit cost (cost of each item produced) is often less than a smaller business can achieve.
- **Financial economies** – large businesses can often obtain funding in the form of loans, overdrafts and credit at lower interest rates than smaller companies.
- **Managerial economies** – division of labour between managers in a large business can be more efficient than one manager in a small business carrying out all the managerial tasks.
- **Marketing economies** – larger businesses spend a lot of money on advertising and promoting their products. Small businesses cannot afford to do this on the same scale.

External economies

- **Infrastructure** – a local authority can feel encouraged to spend money on local roads and other facilities if it knows that a large company (which is likely to employ many local people) will set up in its area. This will be beneficial to both the company itself and the local community.
- **Other benefits to the local economy** – other businesses might also be encouraged to the area. A large well-known retailer, for example, will encourage shoppers into an area. Smaller shops will benefit because shoppers are then likely to come into their shops too.

Diseconomies of scale

Diseconomies of scale occur when a business grows so big that the unit cost of its product or service increases rather than decreases. Although individual causes may vary, this is usually the result of the workforce getting bigger and not having appropriate systems in place to manage people effectively. Reasons often include: poor communication, duplication of effort, slowness or unwillingness to respond to change, and even too many layers of management.

Questions 2

1 **a** Give one advantage of diversification to a business.

b Name two methods by which businesses can diversify.

2 **a** Explain the term 'innovation'.

b How can innovation help a company to keep ahead of its competitors?

c Why is research and development an important element in achieving innovation?

3 Briefly describe what is meant by the terms 'market research' and 'product research'.

4 **a** Give four reasons why a business might want to grow.

b Explain the term 'economies of scale'.

c What is the difference between external and internal economies of scale?

The need to plan

The developers of a project such as the Oblivion ride at Alton Towers would need to ask a range of vital planning questions.

How big will it be? | *When should it be ready?* | *What will it cost?* | *How many workers are needed?* | *What materials are needed?*

Planning is very important. These questions should be answered before a business takes action:

- What product or service will the business produce or provide?
- Should the business produce or provide a new product/service or improve existing ones?
- What forms will the product/service take? Important factors include:
  - design
  - packaging
  - price
  - fitness for purpose.
- What costs will be involved?
- What should the price be set at to cover costs and then bring in a profit?

If planning is done correctly, the following should be the result:

- the product will be well made or the service will be well provided
- the product or service will be competitively priced
- the product or service will suit customers' needs and wants
- the business will not make a loss for too long, if at all
- the product or service will be in demand for as long as possible.

Covering costs

Many new businesses aim simply to cover costs in the first few years until their product or service becomes established. Before starting out, they need to **forecast** their costs and income in advance, for example, for 6–12 months. This will help them calculate if they are likely to cover their costs, and if not, what to do about it. They can do this by producing a cash budget (also called a cash flow statement).

Hint

The cash budget shown on page 33 is made up in advance. It helps a business to project (imagine the future of) its funds.

Planning and control – budgeting and cash flow

Businesses should draw up a **cash budget** as shown below:

Cash budget for June to November

	June £000	July £000	Aug £000	Sep £000	Oct £000	Nov £000
Income	200	400	300	250	400	600
Expenditure	400	400	300	260	500	800

Costs are covered in July and August, because in these months income and expenditure are equal. The business will not have a surplus of cash during these months, but they will break even. In the other months, expenditure is greater than income, so cash is flowing out quicker than cash flowing in, so the business should make arrangements to obtain an overdraft or a short-term loan. They could also request an extension of credit from suppliers.

Having a budget in place helps the owner control cash flow. The budget (or forecast) is therefore a form of planning.

Fixed costs, variable costs and break-even point

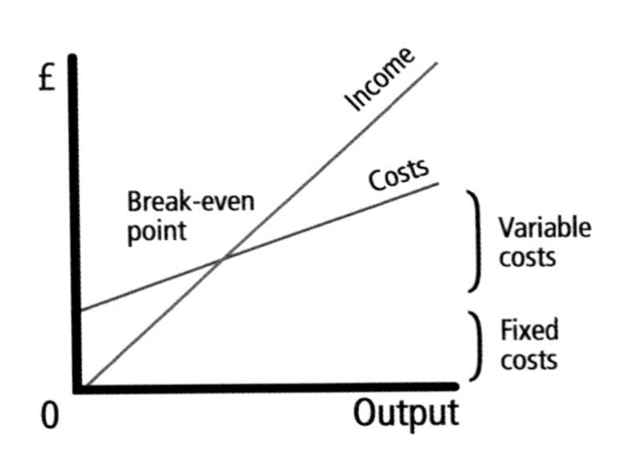

Fixed costs are the costs and expenses which do not change, regardless of how the business is doing, or how many units are being produced (within the relevant time period). Examples include the cost of rent and utilities – these costs remain the same whether production or sales are up or down.

Variable costs are costs and expenses which do vary according to how well the business is doing, or how many units are being produced. If sales are up, then more goods need to be made, so more raw materials need to be bought (and the cost of these may vary further, depending on market prices), and perhaps more staff hired and equipment bought to keep up with increased demand.

The **break-even** point is when income is the same as costs/expenses.

Using final accounts

Businesses produce final accounts at the end of each trading period (usually 12 or 6 months). These are summarised records of how the business performed financially over that period. The main final accounts are the Trading and Profit and Loss Account (often put together) and the Balance sheet.

Trading and Profit and Loss Account

A very simple example is shown on page 34.

The gross profit is the difference between the money received from selling goods and the cost of buying or making these goods. It is a trading profit which is calculated before expenses are deducted.

Trading and Profit and Loss Account of Ellis Island Products Ltd for years 1 and 2		
	Year 1	*Year 2*
	£000	*£000*
Sales turnover	500	700
less Cost of sales	(200)	(300)
Gross profit	**300**	**400**
less Expenses	(160)	(150)
Net profit	**140**	**250**

The net profit is achieved after deducting expenses (sometimes called overheads) from the gross profit. It is the final profit of a company, from which tax is then deducted. Expenses include wages, rent and rates.

Comparing yearly results by calculating and interpreting simple ratios

Ratios can be calculated from final accounts such as the Trading and Profit and Loss Account shown on page 33. This allows for comparisons between years. It helps answer questions such as 'How well has the company done over the 2 years?' and 'Has the business improved or not?'

1 Gross profit % ratio

A higher percentage is desirable, so a company seeks to increase its GP ratio from year to year, not decrease it.

The formula for calculating the gross profit % ratio is: $\frac{\text{gross profit}}{\text{sales}} \times 100$

In the example on page 33, the ratios in years 1 and 2 are:

Year 1: $\frac{300}{500} \times 100 = 60\%$ Year 2: $\frac{400}{700} \times 100 = 57\%$

The ratio has decreased by 3%. This shows that even though the actual gross profit figure has risen, the amount of gross profit for every £ sold has decreased. This is because the cost of sales has increased. Management must look at these increased costs and find reasons for them. If a problem is found, management can act on it before it is too late.

2 Net profit % ratio

The formula for calculating the net profit-to-sales ratio is: $\frac{\text{net profit}}{\text{sales}} \times 100$

In the example on page 33, the ratios in years 1 and 2 are:

Year 1: $\frac{140}{500} \times 100 = 28\%$ Year 2: $\frac{250}{700} \times 100 = 36\%$

The ratio has increased by 8% which is a good sign. It shows that the net profit per £ of products sold has increased over the 2 years. The increase in sales and the slight fall in expenses have contributed to this.

Comparison between companies

In the above example, the business compared its own Trading and Profit and Loss Accounts over 2 years. It could also compare its Trading and Profit and Loss Account with that of another similar company for the same year.

Look at the following example for year 3. Both companies sell the same products, and are approximately the same size. The ratios have already been calculated.

Year 3	Ellis Island Products Ltd		Supergrass Ltd	
		£000		*£000*
Sales turnover		900		850
less Cost of sales		(450)		(350)
Gross profit		**450**		**500**
less Expenses		(200)		(200)
Net profit		**250**		**300**
Gross profit-to-sales ratio	50%		59%	
Net profit-to-sales ratio	28%		35%	

Supergrass Ltd is more efficient in terms of profitability. Despite actual sales being less than Ellis Island's, Supergrass has achieved a higher gross profit for every £ of sales. The same is the case for its net profit ratio. Supergrass's cost of sales figure is smaller than Ellis Island's, so it is paying less for its purchases or production. This suggests that Supergrass is better managed.

Balance sheet

A balance sheet is a 'snapshot' of a business's financial situation on one date at the beginning and/or end of a trading period. It shows the assets and liabilities of a business.

An example of a simple balance sheet is shown below:

Balance sheet of Ellis Island Products Ltd as at 31 January year 1		
	£000	*£000*
Fixed assets		
Premises		200
Vehicles		100
		300
Current assets		
Stock	20	
Debtors	30	
Cash	15	
	65	
Less Current liabilities		
Creditors	30	
Working capital		35
Capital employed		335
As represented by		335
Capital (owner's share in the business)		

Current assets Current assets are items owned by a business for a short time – usually less than a year. They include cash, stock and debtors.

Fixed assets Fixed assets are owned by a business for longer than 1 year and include premises and equipment.

Liabilities Liabilities are amounts of money owed by a business and include short-term loans and creditors.

Working capital The working capital is calculated by deducting current liabilities from current assets. It shows the amount of very liquid assets (e.g. cash and cheques) which a company will have after liabilities are paid off. If there is no working capital, the company could be facing a cash crisis soon.

Capital employed The capital employed is the total capital invested in the business once liabilities have been deducted.

Comparing yearly results by calculating and interpreting simple ratios
Ratios from balance sheets can be used to make comparisons between years and between companies in the same way as those calculated from the Trading and Profit and Loss Accounts on pages 33 and 35.

1 Return on capital employed ratio

The formula for calculating the return on capital employed is: $\frac{\text{net profit}}{\text{capital employed}} \times 100$

The net profit for Ellis Island in year 1 was £140,000 so the return on capital employed is:

$\frac{140}{335} \times 100 = 42\%$

This means that for every £100 invested in the business, less than half (42%) is being returned as profit.

2 Working capital ratio

The formula for calculating the current or working capital ratios is:

current assets : current liabilities

The ratio for Ellis Island can be calculated as follows: $65 : 30 = \frac{65}{30} = 2 : 1$ approximately

This means that for every £1 owed (i.e. liabilities) there are £2 worth of assets to cover them. This is a good sign. There is not too much money tied up in current assets but there is enough to avoid a cash flow crisis.

3 Rate of stock turnover

The formula for calculating the rate of stock turnover is: $\frac{\text{cost of sales}}{\text{average stock}} = ?$ times

This is calculated in two stages:

A Calculating average stock

If stock at the beginning of the trading period was £1000 and at the end it was £900, average stock would be found by adding them (£1900) and dividing by 2 (£950). These figures are found in a trading account.

B Calculating rate of stock turnover

If cost of sales was £1200, then rate of stock turnover is: $\frac{1200}{950} = 1{\cdot}3$ times

If this was calculated on yearly figures, then the above result means that stock is really only shifted once a year. In most businesses this would be a grave cause for concern, but in a small corner shop it would be disastrous. Having a tin of beans on the shelf for a year does not represent good business!

Summary of ratios

Properly used, ratios can tell interested parties about three main areas of a business's finances.

- Profitability – return on capital employed, gross profit to sales, net profit to sales
- Liquidity – working capital ratio
- Efficiency – rate of stock turnover

Questions 3

	Jan *£000*	Feb *£000*	Mar *£000*	Apr *£000*
Income	10	13	15	10
Costs	15	15	15	15

1 a Look at the information above. In which month are costs covered in this business?

b From the words below, choose the correct word to complete this sentence:

The above extract is a forecast. It is, therefore, a form of:

production planning marketing information technology

c The above extract comes from a document which predicts future receipts and payments of cash. What is the name given to this document?

d In the months when costs are not covered, how will the business obtain money to pay for them? Name two methods of obtaining the necessary funds.

e How will the information in this document help the business's owners to control the business's money for the next four months?

Bandbox Ltd

	Year 1 *£000*	Year 2 *£000*
Sales turnover	250	300
less Cost of sales	(100)	(120)
Gross profit	150	180
less Expenses	(50)	(60)
Net profit	£________	£________

2 a What is the name of the final account shown above?

b Calculate net profit for year 1 and year 2.

c (i) Calculate the net profit ratio for both years, showing your working clearly.

(ii) Explain what has happened to the net profit ratio between the two years. Give one possible reason for this, stating whether it is a good or bad indicator for the business. **DM**

d When the company compares its final accounts with that of a rival business, Hatbox, it discovers the following information for year 2:

	Hatbox Ltd	*Bandbox Ltd*
	£000	*£000*
Sales turnover	320	300
less Cost of sales	(211)	(120)
Gross profit	109	180
less Expenses	(80)	(60)
Net profit	29	120
Capital employed	120	140

Which one of the two companies do you think is the better managed? Give reasons for your answer, using ratios where appropriate. **DM**

3 Properly used, ratios tell observers about the three main areas of a business's finances: profitability, liquidity and efficiency. Name, and give formulae for, two ratios which are calculated for profitability, one for liquidity, and one for efficiency.

Why do businesses fail?

Reasons why businesses can fail

There are several reasons why businesses fail:

- competition is too fierce and/or prices are set too high
- the economy is in recession
- there are cash flow problems in the business
- the business is not moving with the times
- poor resource management
- external factors (e.g. war, floods, political factors).

Competition is too fierce

Competition can cause businesses to fail if:

- competitors have a better product (i.e. higher quality or more useful).
- competitors have identified their market more clearly – e.g. a specialist record shop owner realises there is a market for a particular style of music (e.g. dance music) and stocks her shop accordingly. She ignores any records which she does not think will appeal to her specialist market of collectors. She also ignores CDs and tapes, leaving them to other stores, which have different markets.
- competitors set their prices extremely low until the competition is destroyed. This is called destroyer (or predator) pricing. Prices are put back up when the competition is destroyed.
- competitors' costs are lower. They may achieve this by importing goods, parts and resources from countries where wages and production costs are lower.

The economy is in recession

The main features of a recession are that, over a period of time:

- financially, the economy slows down for a period of time
- less is produced, less is spent, less is bought
- obtaining loans is difficult
- unemployment usually increases in a recession.

In this economic climate, many businesses find that sales fall and profits decrease. For businesses with inadequate cash flows and few reserves, it is difficult to survive a long period of recession. Larger businesses and those with reserves of assets should survive until trade improves. However, during a recession, many small businesses do not survive.

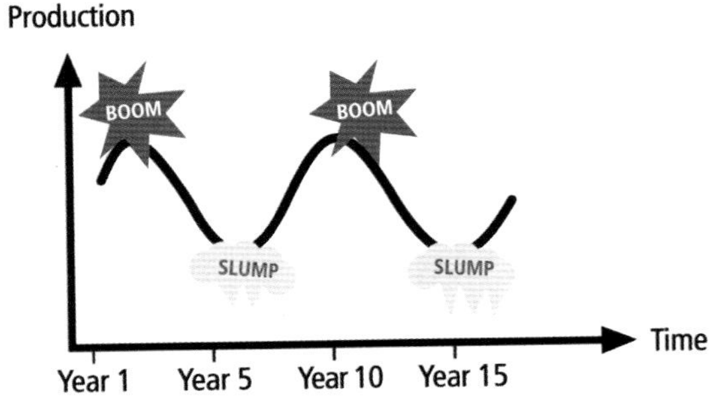

The economy suffers from booms and slumps which occur on a fairly regular basis. A recession is an example of a slump, when production slows down. A boom period is when production increases very rapidly over a period of time. This regular pattern of booms and slumps is sometimes referred to as the **business cycle**.

There are cash flow problems in the business

As shown on pages 32–33, businesses should forecast their need for funds over a period of time (e.g. 6–12 months). They should plan for occasions when money is likely to be short, by arranging overdrafts and loans when needed in advance. They should also plan for problems, e.g. recession, where sales could be poor for a long time. This can be done by keeping reserves of funds, which can be cashed in an emergency. It is not enough to have assets such as premises or equipment. There must also be ready cash to pay day-to-day expenses.

The business is not moving with the times

- Its product is obsolete.
- Its production equipment is outdated; there is a need for automation and technology.
- It (and/or its product) is out of fashion.
- Marketing, advertising and promotion are not effective.
- The product has reached the end of its life cycle and no attempt has been made to extend its lifespan. (See page 89 for information about extending a product's life cycle.)

Analysis of final accounts

CR

Some of the reasons for a firm's problems – and perhaps failure – can be uncovered by analysing the company's accounts. If this analysis is done before the company fails completely, there is a chance of turning the business around.

- **Comparing the gross profit and net profit ratios from year to year**.

  If these fall by a large amount between one year and the next, this could be because of increased costs. The firm should see if these can be decreased. If not, they should calculate whether the increase can be passed on to customers without affecting sales.

- **Comparing gross profit and net profit ratios with those of other companies**.

  This lets the company see whether competition is having an adverse effect. If so, they should see how the company could fight back.

- **Analysing the cash flow**.

  Cash budgets should be analysed in advance to prevent a company from failing to provide appropriate funds when required. This could be done by planning overdrafts and loans for periods when income is likely to be short.

Poor resource management

Some businesses fail because they have managed their resources poorly. The following are examples of poor resource management and their probable effects.

- Supermarket car parks which are poorly maintained could put customers off.
- Shabby paintwork, faulty doors and poorly-heated buildings could also put customers off.
- Equipment and machinery which are badly maintained could cause accidents to staff, as well as lead to inefficient, costly production.
- Lack of efficient security could lead to pilfering and theft.
- Failure to keep accurate records of assets could lead to fraud and theft.
- Poor management of staff could lead to demotivation and staff shortages.
- Prices are set too high. This was a factor in Marks and Spencer's downturn in the early 2000s. High profit margins pushed up prices and made their products less attractive to customers and vulnerable to cheaper competition.

External factors

Businesses can also fail because of factors beyond their control. These will be external to the business. These are summarised as PEST factors:

- **Political** – e.g. new laws or, in extreme situations, declarations of war
- **Economic** – e.g. increases in interest rates can make borrowing more difficult for companies, especially small ones; and for firms who are already in financial difficulty, a rise in interest rates can be the final straw
- **Socio-cultural** – e.g. it is claimed that the ban on smoking in public places (although largely successful) has had an adverse effect on some places like bingo halls, because many bingo players smoke, so the smoking ban has discouraged them from playing, affecting overall business
- **Technological** – e.g. for small firms that produce one or two ranges of products, it is very important that they keep up to date with technological advances, or they will find that their products are outdated and unattractive to the consumer.

More information on these factors is given on pages 75–77.

Socio-cultural Involving both social and cultural factors, that is, how humans participate and behave in structured communities (society) and the shared knowledge and values which help structure these communities (culture).

CASE STUDY: MARKS & SPENCER

Even large and successful companies such as Marks & Spencer can experience difficulties. In the financial year ending 31 March 2001, M&S profits had fallen from more than £1 billion (in 1997/8) to £145 million. Share prices fell by more than two thirds.

There were a number of reasons for this slump.

- M&S experienced the rising costs of using British suppliers. At the same time competitors were importing from low-cost countries. This made selling M&S's selling prices higher than competitors' prices.
- Profit margins in M&S became too high, which pushed up selling prices, and badly affected customer loyalty.
- M&S refused to accept credit cards other than their own.
- The company began losing touch with younger buyers.

In 2004 the company announced a recovery plan, and its fortunes have since improved. However, part of the recovery plan involved a switch from British suppliers to overseas suppliers. British suppliers who had been under contract only to M&S soon found themselves without business, so these businesses failed because of their over-reliance on supplying a single company.

Questions on case study

1 M&S survived, but some of its British suppliers did not. Explain why this was the case.

2 M&S began to import clothing from abroad.

a Give one reason for this.

b What implications do you think this had on prices, and why?

c What implications do you think it had for some British workers in the clothing factories?

Profit margin This is the difference between cost and selling price. If profit margin becomes too high, so does price, and customers will not pay.

Financial year This demonstrates the 12 months in which a company keeps its accounts from year to year. It is not always a calendar year. In the case of M&S, the financial year is from 1 April to 31 March.

Questions 4

1 Pete's Clothing Store has closed down. Along the street, the New Stylez shop attracts buyers looking for designer clothing. Clothes-R-Us sells fashionable clothes at low prices. Pete's shop had neither the advantage of selling exclusive clothes like New Stylez, nor up-to-date fashions like Clothes-R-Us.

Each picture A–D represents a different reason for Pete's failure. From the list below, match a reason to each picture listed in the table. Copy and complete the table. Note that two reasons should be left out.

Reasons

1 Competition from this designer shop was too fierce.
2 There were no parking facilities.
3 Pete's was behind the times compared to this business.
4 Recession in the economy
5 Cash flow problems
6 There was a labour shortage.

Picture	*Reasons*
A New Stylez	
B Clothes-R-Us	
C Newspaper headline	
D Pete's accounts	

2 Competition can have an important part to play in a business's failure. The following practices are undertaken by the competitors of Airjet Limited – a small company which is struggling:

Practice	*Description*
A Destroyer pricing	**1** This involves selling at very low prices to cause the failure of competitors.
B Better quality services and lower prices	**2** Airjet is not moving with the times compared with some of its competitors.
C Newer ideas	**3** This is likely to increase demand for competitors' products because of quality, etc.

Match the practices A–C with the correct descriptions 1–3.

3 The Brent Hotel is a medium-sized, family-run hotel which has been operating for 30 years. Its main competitors are the nearby Royal Hotel and the Burns Hotel. Both of these hotels are thriving while the Brent is struggling.

Of the three hotels, the Brent is the most run-down. The decor in the public rooms has seen better days and the huge, weed-infested grounds are less attractive than the other two. Better parking facilities are required.

The management of the Royal and the Burns Hotels have recognised the importance of providing cut-price packages at weekends when business people do not use the hotels. These reduced rates encourage families and

The Brent Hotel

The Royal Hotel

The Burns Hotel

couples at a time when hotels would be lying empty, like the Brent. The Brent charges the same rates seven days a week, with weekend rates which are much higher than the Royal or the Burns. Their rates for single rooms are also much higher than the other two hotels. The Royal and the Burns have realised that these two areas of pricing have become very important selling points in recent years. Many single travellers now demand better rates, so the Brent loses their custom.

The Brent does not offer conference facilities for business clients, unlike the Royal and the Burns which find these very popular services extremely profitable. It does not have a computer system for bookings, appointments and accounts. The other two hotels do. At the Brent, all of these operations are handwritten by staff and this causes errors, delays and cancelled bookings.

The Brent's profits fell by £30,000 this year. Also, despite having the same number of rooms as the Royal and the Burns Hotels, bookings and profits were only one-third of those gained by the other two hotels. The Brent is suffering from poor resource management, and if improvements are not made, the Brent Hotel might have to close within a year.

a One of the problems for the Brent Hotel is its failure to respond to change. Name three instances of this and state why each of these has affected the hotel's profitability.

b (i) What is meant by the term 'poor resource management'?

(ii) Give three examples of this in the Brent Hotel. Use different examples from part **a** if possible.

c (i) Suggest four improvements which the hotel could make to its current practices. **DM**

(ii) Suggest two ways in which the hotel could promote these improvements to the public. 

What is a successful business?

Measurements of success

Success is measured in different ways. These include the following:

1. achieving profits
2. achieving the aims of the organisation
3. achieving good sales figures
4. having a good relationship with stakeholders (including customers, employees and the local community)
5. being at the forefront of innovation
6. achieving growth
7. providing a good quality product or service
8. having good resource management
9. having a large market share
10. achieving surplus of funds or breaking even

Some or all of points 1–9 are likely to be objectives of most private sector companies. Points 2, 4, 7, 8 and 10 are likely to be objectives of public and voluntary sector organisations.

Different aims of stakeholders

Stakeholders are groups or individuals with an interest in or an influence on an organisation (see also page 14). Stakeholders in a large public limited company include the following:

Stakeholders	*Interest/influence in company*
Managing director	Large profits, growth, size of salary, career potential, returns to personal shareholding and to shareholders, welfare of the workforce, outside issues (e.g. environment and local community), competitors, innovation, costs
Senior management	Similar to managing director's
Shareholders	Large profits, value of shares, large dividends, stability of the company, stability of the economy, moral/ethical issues
Existing and potential creditors	Payment of money owed to them, reassurance that the company is stable and solvent
Employees	Stability and security of the organisation (which will affect the security of their jobs), career potential, profits
Customers	Quality of product or service, price, delivery, after sales service, ethical and health issues
Suppliers	Payment, stability, solvency
Local community	Provision of jobs, environmental issues (e.g. car parking and pollution)
Local authority	Provision of jobs for local community, taxes from the company, sponsorship

Competing aims of stakeholders

CR

Some of these aims compete with one another. For example, the profit-making aims of the first four stakeholders listed above may not be wholly compatible with the wishes of customers who want low prices.

Another conflict could arise between the managing director's wish for innovation and the job security which employees want. Innovation might include the introduction of automation and new production techniques which could result in job losses. Job losses will also be in conflict with the wishes of the local authority. The innovation could, however, be in the interests of customers – the new technology may lead to lower prices because unit costs will be cut.

Questions 5

1 Success means different things to different organisations.

a Give one example of an organisation in each sector listed below. An example has been given for the first one. Provide another example for this sector.

(i) public sector: e.g. fire service, ________________

(ii) private sector: e.g. ________________

(iii) voluntary sector: e.g. ________________

b (i) For each of the organisations listed in part a, give two ways in which each one measures success.

(ii) Are the measures of success different in each sector?

(iii) If the answer to part (ii) is yes, give reasons for this.

2 Some stakeholders in Optics plc are: shareholders, suppliers, local residents, and customers.

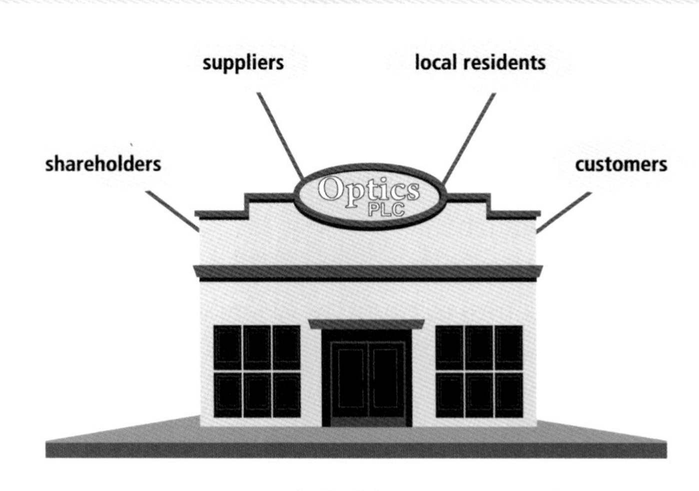

Some stakeholders in Optics plc

a A shareholder is interested in the progress of Optics plc in which she invests. What do you think her main aim for herself and the company will be?

b Describe one main aim of the customers of Optics plc which would compete with the main aim of the shareholder stated in part **a** above.

c Local residents are petitioning Optics plc to build better parking facilities in its grounds. At present, many employees park in the streets. Suppliers' lorries also have to off-load supplies in the streets. Residents complain that this causes congestion, a high level of exhaust fumes in a residential area, and danger to local children crossing streets. Residents also have difficulty in parking outside their own homes. If Optics plc agrees to their demands, the residents will benefit but other stakeholders might not.

(i) State which stakeholders shown in the diagram might not benefit from this action in the short term. Give reasons.

(ii) If the company does not take action, the residents will continue to experience the social costs of having Optics plc in their neighbourhood. State what these social costs are.

CHAPTER 3
WHAT RESOURCES DO BUSINESSES USE?

Why do businesses locate where they do?

Factors influencing the location of businesses

The following factors can influence the location of businesses:

- nearness to markets for selling products and services
- proximity to good infrastructure such as roads and railways to enable customers to come in, and/or allow easy transport of products out
- costs of land, premises, etc. on which to build shops and/or factories
- car parking facilities for workers and/or customers
- nearness to raw materials, e.g. fishing fleets in Scotland are mostly located north and west where the best fish stocks are found
- availability of labour
- costs of labour: a recent trend has been to outsource some operations (like call centres) to countries where wages are cheaper than in the UK, e.g. India.

Consider the following example. Where will the owner open his shop?

Sensible places

- Nearness to markets – where many customers live and/or go shopping, e.g. in a town or city.
- Away from the competition – in a part of town where there are few (if any) pet shops, but where there will still be demand.
- Reasonable costs – in a part of town where costs of land, premises and taxes are not too high.
- Near to good infrastructure – main road and rail links nearby will help customers and suppliers to get there.
- Car parking – nearby car parking would also be helpful.

Unwise places

- Remote areas – pet owners are unlikely to travel far for a small shop.
- Very near competition – in a road with five similar shops.
- A very expensive part of town – where costs are likely to be higher than profits.
- Far from good infrastructure – if access is difficult, customers are unlikely to come in large numbers. Also, if suppliers find access difficult, their prices will become higher.

CASE STUDY: TESCO

Tesco plc is an international grocery and general merchandising retail chain based in Great Britain. It is the UK's largest retailer by both global sales and domestic market.

Its location policy in the UK is to locate different sizes and types of stores in locations that suit each type of store. They also aim to suit the needs of customers working or living in these locations.

Tesco's policy, therefore, is not to limit itself to one type of location, but to choose many different ones, and provide shops and services that suit each location. This is shown in the table below. The stores are shown in order of size with the largest first.

Brand name	*Size and type of store*	*Typical features*	*Typical locations*
Tesco Extra	Hypermarkets; approx. 60,000 sq ft	Large variety of goods including clothing and electronics	Out of town/edge of town, space for large free carparks
Tesco Superstore	Supermarket; approx. 20,000–50,000 sq ft	Food and non-food items such as books and DVDs	Suburbs, edge of town
Tesco Metro	Small supermarket; 7000–15,000 sq ft	Mainly food, especially packaged and prepared foods	City centre; high streets of small town
Tesco Express	Convenience shops up to 3000 sq ft	Mainly food and drinks	Petrol station forecourts, busy city centre districts, small shopping precincts

Questions on case study

1. State three differences between Tesco Extra and Tesco Express stores.
2. By providing a wide range of locations, and various types of stores, Tesco has become very competitive against other retailers. Why do you think this is?

Infrastructure

Infrastructure is the system of structures and facilities which make business activity easier. Examples include: roads; railways; air travel facilities, e.g. airports; schools and colleges for training future staff; and hospitals.

Roads and other travel facilities are important because:

- they allow products and materials into the business effectively
- they allow products out of the business easily
- they provide easy access for customers
- they make it easier for branches and other businesses in different parts of the country or world to have meetings.

'Nearness to markets' can refer to local customers, but if the infrastructure is of high quality, it should also be possible to reach European and other markets quickly by road, rail or air.

Schools, colleges and hospitals are important in providing for the education, development and welfare (when required) of staff and users of the services. Utilities such as gas, water and electricity are also important. Businesses are unlikely to locate in areas which do not provide these facilities.

Where does the finance for locating come from?

There are many different sources of finance, as shown in the following diagram:

loans from friends, debenture holders

owners – capital, shares

EU funding for member countries, e.g. in areas of high unemployment

credit from suppliers – buy now, pay later

loans and hire purchase from banks and other finance companies

overdrafts from banks

grants from government and local authorities for locating in certain areas, e.g. with high unemployment

Sources of finance

Businesses can get finances from a number of sources:

- they can get an **overdraft**, which is an agreed level of debt provided by a bank. It is often a flexible amount, up to an agreed limit, with a flexible timescale, usually intended as short-term funding (1 year or less).
- they can get a **loan**, which is a fixed amount of borrowed money, usually supplied by a bank. It has a fixed timescale (which can be renegotiated and extended), and is usually intended as long-term funding (longer than 1 year).

As a business grows, it might also receive money from the following sources:

- **shareholders** who invest money in the business by buying shares in it. If the business makes a profit, these shareholders normally receive some of the profit in the form of dividends. Those holding preference shares usually receive dividends first. If there are funds left, the ordinary shareholders are then entitled to dividends at a higher rate because of the greater risk. (Dividends are a part of the company's profit and are paid to shareholders once or twice a year.)
- **debenture holders** who provide money in the form of investment loans and are entitled to receive interest from the company.

The business must be a limited company or a plc to have shareholders. It must be a plc to receive money from debenture holders.

Internet research

Visit the Business Link website. In the section on finance and grants, there is information about borrowing. Take some notes on the advantages and disadvantages of loans and overdrafts.

Links to this site and other websites relating to Standard Grade Business Management can be found at: **www.leckieandleckie.co.uk** by clicking on the Learning Lab button and navigating to the Standard Grade Business Management Course Notes page.

Government assistance

Assistance from Scottish Government and/or UK Government

The Scottish Executive was established by the Scotland Act 1998. It is now known as the Scottish Government, and has responsibility for health, education, justice, rural affairs and transport in Scotland. There are, however, a large number of matters that the UK Government (i.e. at Westminster) is responsible for, in the UK as a whole, including defence, foreign policy, etc. Both governments provide assistance to business.

The authorities offer assistance to businesses by providing:

- training through Local Enterprise Companies in Scotland (LECs), and Local Learning and Skills Councils (LLSCs) in England. These are government funded to foster local economic growth and development. They also aim to encourage investment in certain areas.
- New Enterprise Scholarships (NECs) for new entrepreneurs in disadvantaged areas
- Regional Development Agencies (RDAs) in England
- financial assistance such as:
  - Selective Finance for Investment (SFI) in England
  - Regional Selective Assistance (RSA) in Scotland
- Assisted areas: to qualify for RSA grants, companies must fulfil certain criteria, such as being located in assisted areas. These are areas of high unemployment.

Authorities provide this assistance because they want to increase levels of business and enterprise, reduce unemployment levels, and make better use of derelict land. Crime rates are often linked to deprivation and poverty which are other factors influencing governments.

Hint

Terms used by governments can change, so check the above terms regularly for updates. If you use a search engine to look up these terms on the internet you will find websites that give you more information about them. The Department of Business, Enterprise and Regulatory Reform and RSA Scotland have helpful websites.

CASE STUDY: MCCALLUM BAGPIPES

McCallum Bagpipes Ltd manufactures Scottish bagpipes and accessories. It is based in Kilmarnock, Scotland, and was established in 1998. In November 2002, the company was offered Regional Selective Assistance of £13,000 to expand its business, and to broaden its customer base by producing new types of bagpipes such as Spanish pipes. RSA assisted with project costs of £61,000 and helped create 5.5 new jobs. The company has subsequently grown and total employment now stands at over 20.

Questions on case study

1. Do you think that Kilmarnock is in an assisted area? Give a reason for your answer.
2. Why do the Scottish Government and central government encourage businesses to move to assisted areas?
3. Do you think McCallum Bagpipes has earned its RSA grant? Give a reason for your answer.

Local government

Local authorities in the UK try to promote their area and encourage businesses to set up in it. This can be done by:

- advertising on the internet, in newspapers, magazines and on television
- giving detailed information to businesses about getting the relevant grants and other aid
- giving detailed information to businesses about local sites and premises
- providing grants for starting up a business in their local area
- providing grants for research and development.

Internet research

Look up your local government website, and note down what type of assistance it offers to local businesses.

Links to this site and other websites relating to Standard Grade Business Management can be found at: **www.leckieandleckie.co.uk** by clicking on the Learning Lab button and navigating to the Standard Grade Business Management Course Notes page.

European Union

The European Union (EU), which consists of 27 European countries as of 1 January 2007, provides one market of over 490 million potential customers with very few, if any, restrictions between member countries. This is often referred to as the Single Market.

Advantages of being a member of the EU include:

- no **quotas** (maximum limits) between member countries, which means that member countries are not limited to a quota for the goods that they want to sell in other member countries
- no customs duties between member countries
- free movement of workers and capital between member countries
- larger choice of suppliers
- businesses might be more prepared to pay the high costs required for

research and development if they have a large, unrestricted market in Europe (economies of scale)
- increase in competition, which should increase efficiency
- procedures for moving products around Europe should be simplified – fewer regulations and less paperwork
- restrictive practices (such as government subsidies and tariffs) stopped.

Disadvantages of being a member of the EU include:

- language barriers and cultural differences
- distance problems and different trading hours
- currency difficulties in the short term
- bottlenecks in production due to large demand.

EU funding can help businesses in certain areas. Funding is sometimes given for projects such as:

- road building
- redevelopment of derelict inner city areas
- development of other infrastructure (e.g. schools and hospitals).

This help is often aimed at reducing unemployment. The EU provides structural funds to help in the above activities. Three of these are:

- the **European Social Fund** – provides financial aid for projects which will improve training and job prospects
- the **European Regional Development Fund** – provides financial aid for businesses involved in infrastructure (e.g. road building) and telecommunication projects.
- the **European Agricultural Guidance and Guarantee Fund** – provides job opportunities in farming areas.

Some non-EU companies, such as those from Japan and the USA, have set up businesses in EU countries in order to gain some of these benefits. This can bring benefits to local EU areas in the form of employment, higher spending power, increased standard of living and prosperity in depressed areas where these businesses set up.

The **euro** (symbol €) is the official currency of many European countries. Most members of the European Union have adopted the euro as their currency (replacing individual national currencies), although Great Britain, Denmark and Sweden have opted out of the euro. The adoption of a single currency makes it easier for organisations to do business within Europe (the 'Eurozone'), as they do not need to convert between currencies or risk fluctuations in value.

Globalisation

Owing to the vast improvements in links between countries, like transport and communications, the world is fast becoming one big marketplace. The terms **global market** and **globalisation** are often used to describe this. Examples of such links are shown in the table on page 52.

Type	Examples
ICT (informaton and communication technology)	Satellite, cable, mobile phones, world wide web
Transport	Containerisation, infrastructure for roads, rail, air
Trade agreements	Relaxation of trade barriers, e.g. EU

Multinationals

Some businesses are very large, and produce, distribute and advertise their goods and services all over the world. This is an example of globalisation. Features of globalisation include:

- using the same brand name in all countries (i.e. a global brand)
- using the same advertising in all countries
- using the same procedures and practices in all countries.

These businesses are called **multinational** companies. Pepsi is an example of a global brand which uses the same advertising and packaging throughout the world. In some countries, such as India and China, where people now earn more, these branded goods can give the buyer added social status.

Multinationals have branches in many different countries. They often begin in one country but then see advantages in producing in some or all of the countries where their products are sold. This often reduces transport and wage costs. Nearness to markets and the receipt of local government grants are other possible advantages.

Importance of ICT in globalisation

ICT enables information to be transmitted very quickly to and from customers worldwide via the world wide web. For example, in some airlines, staff across the globe are trained to sell any ticket in any country.

In these cases, the use of ICT means that relocation of staff and other resources is not necessary. ICT, therefore, allows staff and equipment to remain where they are. However, they can interact with staff in other locations through the use of new technology.

Word-processor operators in India produce documents for some executives in the USA because:

- word-processor operators earn much less in India than in the USA
- ICT enables the information to be transmitted and the documents received very quickly between the countries.

Advantages of globalisation

- Vast market of consumers
- Reduction in some trade and cultural barriers
- Communications are easier and quicker via internet and phone systems
- Better awareness of how to deal with businesses and customers in other areas
- Increased choice of resources

Disadvantages of globalisation

There can be communication problems between branches in different countries due to:

- language difficulties
- culture differences
- different time zones
- technological failure.

Other problems can include:

- different tax laws in different countries
- different consumer regulations and standards
- currency differences (the euro might help solve this problem in Europe).

Questions 1

1 **a** Look at the picture on the right. List three things which might have encouraged Donny to open an ice-cream shop there.

b Donny needs more money because he wants to extend his premises. Name two possible sources of financial capital which might be available to him.

c The government sometimes helps businesses to set up new premises in certain areas. Which areas are likely to receive the most assistance and why?

CR

d What kind of assistance does the EU give to help reduce unemployment and factory closures in the UK?

e Explain the term 'multinational company'. What factors will influence where it locates its business, and what problems is it likely to face once it has located abroad?

2 A medium-sized car manufacturing company is about to locate in the north of England. The owners decide to build the factory near a town with high unemployment levels. Name four sources of finance which might be available to the owners for this purpose.

3 When identifying possible locations for a business, its owners have to consider a number of factors, such as: availability of raw materials, distance to the market, availability of labour, availability of land, transport costs, infrastructure.

Choose three of these six factors. For each factor chosen, describe the type of business which might find it the most important location factor.

4 If a company sets up business in an EU country, it will find that the Single Market has many advantages.

a Briefly explain the term Single Market.

b Name and briefly describe three advantages which the Single Market brings to a business which locates in an EU country.

c Give two disadvantages of the Single Market.

d What advantages are there for:

(i) non-EU companies which set up in the EU

(ii) the areas in which they set up in business?

Why people work

Different people work for different reasons, including:

- to make money
- for job satisfaction
- for security
- for companionship and friendship
- to make progress or use their abilities and talents.

Choosing the right person for the job

A person's qualities should fit the job.

A zoo-keeper and a medical consultant will need different qualities.

Qualities for a zoo-keeper might include the following:

- experience with animals
- scientific knowledge
- patience
- good physical fitness
- being safety conscious.
- love of animals
- being observant

Qualities for a medical consultant might include the following:

- appropriate degree
- patience
- ability to take responsibility
- additional qualification to reach consultant status
- experience in hospitals
- interpersonal skills

Internet research

Visit the Learn Direct website. This site lists over 700 different types of jobs and their requirements. Try to find out the kind of work that zoo-keepers do.

Links to this site and other websites relating to Standard Grade Business Management can be found at: **www.leckieandleckie.co.uk** by clicking on the Learning Lab button and navigating to the Standard Grade Business Management Course Notes page.

Job training

- **On-the-job training** occurs in the workplace.
- **Off-the-job training** occurs outside the workplace, at a local college or training centre.
- **Apprenticeship** occurs mostly in the workplace but there can be some external training such as one day a week at a training centre or college.
- **Induction** training usually occurs when someone starts a new job, especially if he or she is completely new to the organisation. This helps

the employee settle in. It shows the employee how the business works generally, lets him or her meet people, and gives some on-the-job training.

- **Retraining** means training for a completely new occupation, e.g. from mechanic to computer analyst.
- **Upgrading training** means becoming trained in new skills for an existing job. This often occurs when computer operators have to become acquainted with new hardware and/or software packages.

The salary level is often affected by the amount of training required and the level of responsibility in the job. Scarcity is also another factor which affects salary level. This is one reason why top film stars and entertainers can obtain such high fees.

Hours worked

- **Full-time** usually means working every weekday from around 9 am until 5 pm (or equivalent). Full-time work can be permanent or temporary.
- **Part-time** means working for only part of the week. Examples include working two days each week, or mornings only for five days a week. Part-time work can be permanent or temporary.
- **Permanent** work is where a job lasts as long as the company is in business, provided the person is not sacked or made redundant. It can be full-time or part-time.
- **Temporary** work lasts for a limited time which can range from 2–3 days to several years. It might be seasonal work, such as fruit-picking, or work for a set time such as maternity cover. It can be full-time or part-time.

Work patterns

Where and when people work varies much more than it did previously. The impact of ICT and the wish to create a better work–life balance means that businesses and employees are now looking to establish more flexible working patterns.

- **Contract**: employees are now given contracts which may be permanent or temporary, full-time or permanent.
- **Fixed-term contract**: a fixed-term contract has specified start and finish dates; often used by businesses when particular skills and expertise are needed for specific projects or to get through a particularly busy period.
- **Flexitime**: employees arrange their own work hours, starting and finishing at times to suit them and their commitments (although they normally work 'core' hours); they can work longer days, building up extra hours, enabling them to take off time at a later date (instead of taking annual leave).
- **Job share**: when one full-time job is shared between two people (that is, each person works part-time, but combined they do a full job). Salary, holidays and other terms are shared in proportion to the number of hours each person works.
- **Casual**: when employees are taken on for occasional short periods of time, usually to do unskilled work, at times of increased business activity when the regular workforce can't cope.

- **Shift work**: when employees work at different times of the day or night, to ensure that the organisation is always operational. This may be needed to provide a service (as in an accident and emergency department in a hospital) or to ensure machines are not left idle when they could be making goods.

Types of workers

There are four basic categories of worker:

- **manual workers**: unskilled labour
- **blue collar workers**: semi-skilled labour who often perform repetitive tasks, for example factory workers
- **white collar workers**: skilled labour, for example, sales assistants
- **professionals**: for example, doctors, lawyers, teachers, engineers.

Job specification/description

A job specification gives details about a job. These details will include some or all of the following:

- job title
- department
- brief job description
- main duties of the job
- job responsibilities
- working conditions.

A job specification tells job applicants what the job will entail. It also gives employers some idea of the type of person required to fill the position.

Person specification

Once a job specification has been drawn up, employers should make up a list of attributes which they expect from the person who will fill the position. This list will be included in a person specification. Some attributes will be essential and some will be desirable. An example of a person specification is given below.

Qualities/qualifications	*Essential*	*Desirable*
Enthusiasm	☐	☐
Initiative	☐	☐
Excellent communications skills	☐	☐
Honours degree	☐	☐
Driving licence	☐	☐
Previous experience	☐	☐
Ability/willingness to work overtime	☐	☐
Ability to supervise a team	☐	☐
Excellent interactive skills	☐	☐
ICT skills	☐	☐

Employers will tick the essential or desirable column for each quality or qualification. If a standard form is used for all jobs in the business, some qualities and qualifications may not be relevant to certain jobs. Therefore, they can be left blank or 'not applicable' can be inserted where appropriate.

Selection and recruitment

When a business wishes to employ staff (either to fill a vacancy or create new posts), it usually takes the following steps.

1 The business advertises the post – either externally or internally.

External advertising	*Internal advertising*
Using ICT – on the business's website, the internet or via teletext In the media – in newspapers and magazines Using agencies – job centres and employment agencies will advertise jobs; some will also carry out interviews	Methods include: • memos • staff bulletins • notice-boards • email • intranet • staff announcements

2 The job advertisement usually tells applicants what to do next. This will normally involve:
   - sending in a letter of application with a curriculum vitae (CV), or
   - requesting an application form (e.g. by phone, letter), then completing and returning it by a due date.

References are usually required with either method.

3 The business sends out application forms if applicable.

4 The business receives applications.

5 The applications are all studied and checked against job specifications and person specifications.

6 A short list of applicants who seem most suitable (on paper) for the job is made up.

7 Interviews and proficiency tests are arranged and carried out.

8 The final candidate is chosen and offered the position.

9 Within 13 weeks of starting work, a new employee must be given a Contract of Employment which includes the following information:
   - job title and description/responsibilities
   - date job commenced
   - hours of work
   - rate and method of pay
   - period of notice to be given
   - holiday arrangements
   - pension scheme arrangements
   - rights concerning trade unions
   - the organisation's disciplinary procedures.

Appraisal

CR

Informal staff appraisal involves the subjective evaluation of staff's performance by their manager. It relies on the feelings of others. There are no agreed criteria and there is little structure. It is usually not discussed with staff.

Formal staff appraisal has the following characteristics:

- appraisals are carried out regularly (e.g. yearly or twice yearly)
- appraisals are usually carried out by supervisors/managers for their subordinates, but can be done by peer groups or by oneself
- appraisal forms are used to provide a record of the appraisal
- appraisals can involve grading, which can affect the employee's promotion prospects
- work performance is usually matched against job description.

Appraisal is a form of monitoring.

- It checks a person's general suitability for the job.
- It monitors a person's suitability for promotion.
- It allows for a person's ambitions to be recognised and accounted for.
- It helps motivate.
- It helps identify training needs.
- It identifies strengths and weaknesses of staff.

A successful staff appraisal:

- sets targets agreed by both the appraiser and appraisee (setting timescales and making decisions on work to be done). Target-setting helps measure performance.
- recognises the employee's achievements
- identifies difficulties
- is objective
- identifies skills the employee needs to develop if they are to progress
- creates two-way communication between employers and employees.

Advantages and disadvantages of appraisal

Advantages	Disadvantages
Positive feedback increases motivation	Could cause job specification to be altered, which may increase workload
Encourages employees to build on strengths	Negative feedback could be discouraging to workers if not tactfully handled
Identifies training needs and promotion pathways	

Interrelationship between employers and employees

- Two-way communication is important.
- Understanding of each other's job can be helpful.
- Accountability should be recognised by both employers and employees.
- Teamwork is important.
- Training courses can be important for both employers and employees.

Legislation

Legislation also affects the relationship between employers and employees. The following Acts of Parliament lay down rules for the workplace:

- The Disabled Persons (Employment) Acts 1944 and 1958
- The Factories Act 1961
- Offices, Shops and Railway Premises Act 1963
- The Equal Pay Act 1970
- Contract of Employment Act 1972
- Health and Safety at Work Act 1974
- The Sex Discrimination Acts 1975 and 1985
- The Race Relations Act 1976
- Disability Discrimination Act 1995
- The National Minimum Wage Act 1998.

Hint

You are not expected to know full details of these Acts, but you may find it helpful to know: the names of some of the Acts, what some of them contain and how laws can affect a business.

Trade unions

A trade union is an organisation that represents employees and workers. The main aim of a trade union is to improve the working terms and conditions of its members (wages, conditions such as annual leave, sickness benefits and dismissal, and other work-related issues). A trade union will negotiate these matters with employers on behalf of workers, and their strength and power lie in their size. There are different trade unions for different groups of workers. For example, Unison Scotland represents members working in public and related services in Scotland.

Industrial action

If relations between employers and employees break down, employees may decide to take part in industrial action which can take the following forms:

- **picketing** – union members stand outside their own business's entrance trying to persuade other workers not to cross the picket line. Standing outside another business for this reason is illegal.
- **go-slow** – workers deliberately slow down their work rate
- **work-to-rule** – the job is followed strictly by the letter of the contract; sometimes the work is slowed down as a result
- **overtime ban** – workers refuse to work any extra hours over their contract hours
- **strike** – workers completely withdraw their labour for a period of time.

ACAS – the Advisory, Conciliation and Arbitration Service – is an independent organisation, funded by central government, which works with businesses and workers to improve employment relations and therefore performance. It is called on for advice and arbitration (judgement) when employees and employers cannot resolve disputes themselves.

To avoid poor relations, businesses may encourage employees to participate more actively in the business through:

- **Team working** – Employees are involved in setting targets. This might involve a team deciding that 500 units can be produced by them each day. Since they set the target, not management, it is more likely to be reached. They participate in the decision-making process.
- **Quality circles** – Employees pool their experience and specialist knowledge to study problems and suggest solutions. This helps create a feeling of worth and increases motivation.
- **Works councils** – Employees and managers work together to discuss working conditions, and agree or amend suggested changes, especially significant ones, before they are rolled out in the organisation.

Changing employment patterns

- Many large businesses employ large numbers of temporary staff. In some cases as many as 25% (one quarter) of staff can be temporary, i.e. they can leave (or lose) their jobs at any time.
- Many jobs are now on specific contracts for limited periods – usually until a particular job is completed. Actors on a film, for example, work under contract until the project (i.e. the film) is completed.
- In Britain, many jobs have moved from the manufacturing sector to the service sector (i.e. from secondary to tertiary industry). For example, many more people work in insurance, banking and tourism than in car manufacturing and house building. The UK has always had a strong service sector, but it has recently become dominant because of the massive decline in the old manufacturing industries. These included shipbuilding, coal mining and steel making. Manufacturing industries which do still exist need far fewer workers due to advances in automation and technology.
- ICT is enabling more people to work full-time or part-time from home, or in transit, than ever before, either on an employed or self-employed basis.
- ICT is also changing the pattern of employment in the workplace – fewer people, more technology.
- The balance between female and male workers is changing – many more females are working than was the case in previous years.
- Important employment terms include:
  - **core workers** – usually full-time, permanent members of staff whose skills and expertise are vital to the organisation
  - **casual workers** – temporary staff who are only employed when needed. They have no job security.
  - **job sharing** – two or more workers split a job between them. Work space, resources and tasks are shared, as are salary, annual leave and other conditions of employment.
  - **flexitime** – employees arrange their own work hours, starting and finishing at times to suit them and their commitments; they usually have to work around a core set of hours (for example, from 10 am until 2 pm); they can work longer days, building up extra hours, enabling them to take off time later.

- **homeworking** – when an employee does their job from their own home, rather than in the organisation's premises or office. This is usually facilitated by the use of ICT equipment.
- **teleworking** – when an employee does their job away from the organisation's premises with the use of ICT equipment

Advantages of flexible work patterns to employee include:	**Disadvantages of flexible work patterns to employee include:**
less money and time spent on travel	lack of social contact
can arrange hours to suit own needs	may feel excluded from decision-making processes
Advantages of flexible work patterns to employer include:	**Disadvantages of flexible work patterns to employer include:**
better retention of valued staff because they are more content	potential difficulties with communication and/or supervision
more productive staff	can be difficult to provide ICT equipment and support

Questions 2

1 The local sports centre has a vacancy. The job entails the supervision and teaching of swimming classes three mornings per week. Travelling to several other sports centres will be necessary at least once a week and occasionally in the evenings. There will be some paperwork and administration involved, and working with other people will occur at regular intervals.

Copy and complete the person specification below, ticking which qualities or qualifications you consider essential for the job or desirable for the job. Leave blank any qualities or qualifications which you do not think are essential or desirable for this particular job.

Person specification

Qualities/Qualifications	Essential	Desirable
Life-saving qualification		
Driving licence		
Honours degree		
Previous experience		
Ability to supervise a team		
Enthusiasm		
Excellent interactive skills (i.e. can get on with people)		
Some clerical skills		
Knowledge of local area		
First aid certificate		
Experience of working with animals		
Punctuality		
Ability to swim		

2 Digitz Ltd is a medium-sized business producing components for computers. It has operated a successful formal staff appraisal system for four years.

- **a** Write a paragraph explaining what is meant by staff appraisal, showing clearly the difference between informal and formal appraisal.
- **b** List five features of a successful staff appraisal.
- **c** For both managers and staff, describe:
  - (i) the positive aspects of appraisal
  - (ii) the negative aspects of appraisal.
- **d** What is target-setting and why is it important in any staff appraisal system?

3 Businesses can only be successful if the relationship between employees and employers are clearly defined and understood by both.

- **a** Name five pieces of legislation which affect employees in their place of work.
- **b** (i) When a new employee is taken on, what must he or she be given within 13 weeks of starting work?
  - (ii) State four things which this item should include.
- **c** If the relationship between employers and employees breaks down, industrial action can occur. Name and briefly describe four types of industrial action which can be taken by employees.
- **d** One way of avoiding strained relationships between management and staff is to encourage employee participation. Name and describe two examples of this.

How do businesses use information?

What is information?

Information is data that helps us in day-to-day living. For example:

- it is important to know where to buy our food
- it is important to know whom to phone in emergencies, e.g. fire, police, ambulance
- it is important to know where the school is so we can go there to learn.

The information given above is usually given verbally. Parents, teachers, friends and others tell us this information.

Giving and receiving information is also vital to businesses, and can be transmitted in a number of ways. It can be:

- **verbal** – phone calls/voice mail/answering machine, directly by word of mouth, e.g. sales representatives
- **written** – letters, memos, notices, reference books such as the telephone book and dictionaries
- **numerical** – spreadsheets and tables of data and information, such as employees' wages, monthly sales figures, trading and profit and loss accounts

- **graphical/pictorial** – graphs and charts such as bar charts, line graphs, pie charts and pictograms (often showing numerical data in pictorial format), presentations, posters, illustrations
- **electronic** – email, internet, teletext, telephone, fax, computer databases and spreadsheets. Information which is transmitted by technology can be given on screen and/or on paper and/or verbally (e.g. telephone and videoconferencing).

Information comes from a large range of sources – employees, customers, suppliers, competitors, researchers, retailers and media.

Good information is very important

The following scenarios show that custom can be lost if businesses do not communicate quickly and correctly with their customers:

1. A customer phones a company and is put on hold for ten minutes, after being talked to quite rudely. The customer becomes impatient, puts the phone down, and uses another company. The customer is unlikely to contact the first company again, and will also probably recommend others not to.
2. A customer gets through but cannot be given the information requested. Again the customer is likely to behave as in scenario 1 above.
3. A customer obtains the required information but it turns out to be wrong. For example, the price quoted should have been £1050 not the £105 which was given to the customer. The customer is unlikely to pay up when the mistake is discovered. The result is that the business loses the difference, which is not good for profits!

It is clear that information should be given swiftly, accurately, efficiently and politely. This will help to win and retain customers, suppliers and other interested stakeholders of the organisation.

Internal and external information

Internal information is information about the business that is available within the business, and is contained in items such as:

- sales reports
- final accounts
- database files
- staff appraisals
- word processing documents
- memorandums.

External information is the information found or contained in items generated outwith the business, such as: government statistics, product reports in magazines, articles in newspapers about the business, and articles on the internet about consumer spending.

Managers use internal and external information to help make decisions. For example, if a sales report shows that a particular sales representative's sales figures are down, the sales manager may question the sales rep and find out that customers prefer the competition's product because it is endorsed by a celebrity. The sales manager may use this information to get a different celebrity to endorse their product.

A social services manager in a local authority may use government statistics on the number of teenagers in their area to decide where to locate a new drop-in leisure and recreation centre, and how large it needs to be.

Information and communication

To ensure the efficiency of the business, employees should be very clear about what is required of them, and employers should know what employees are doing. If the information in the following sources is accurate and up-to-date, communication within the business should be clear and effective:

- job specifications
- regular meetings
- memorandums
- verbal communications to and from management
- notices
- handbooks
- internal email.

If these provide the appropriate information clearly, everyone should know what is expected of them.

Evaluation of information

CR

Businesses must decide:

- what information is relevant to them
- which information is most important to them
- what the information means
- how it can be used to avoid problems in the future
- how it can be used to ensure continued success.

Information should be accurate, complete, on time, easily understood and cost-effective.

The type of information which can be evaluated includes: accounts, worker performance and production.

Accounts

- comparison of profits between years
- comparison of profits with that of competitors
- monitoring sales volume, i.e. the number sold and the sales value (prices of goods)
- checking for fraud
- checking if the company improved its market share over the past few years
- checking if profit-to-sales ratios increased or decreased.

Worker performance

- appraisals
- employees' progress reports
- sales volume and profits per department
- customer evaluations
- staff motivation–checking what improvements can be made.

Production

- checking whether targets were reached
- checking the reasons for wastage
- mechanical or technological reports.

The above information is more likely to be written rather than verbal. This written information will be scrutinised in order to check the efficiency of different sections of the business, and look for areas which are operating well, and those which need improvement. The above points will have to be checked and resolved.

Monitoring and controlling

Evaluating information helps businesses to monitor and control. This means keeping a regular eye on important information. If changes occur (bad or good), managers should:

- know as soon as possible
- find out reasons for the changes
- decide whether to take action.

The last step involves controlling.

When monitoring and controlling take place, the following questions are likely to be asked:

- Are procedures being followed?
- Are they working? If not, what changes should be made?
- What is working well? How can it be continued?
- What needs fixing? How can it be sorted?
- What constraints are there? How can the business overcome them, or work within them?

Software applications

Computer software can record and produce vast amounts of information. This information can help managers in their decision making. The key applications used in businesses are:

- **Word processing** – mainly used for producing text-based documents such as reports, letters, memos, etc.
- **Database** – electronic filing systems used for customer records, staff records, stock control, telephone numbers, etc.
- **Spreadsheet** – mainly used for recording figures and making calculations, e.g. stock records, simple accounts and cash flow; also makes charts and graphs.

The following table gives examples of information and decision making which are made easier by software applications.

ICT application	*Functional area*	*Content*	*Decision made*
Word processing	Finance	Letter informing customer her loan is paid off	Send leaflets to customer about new loan deals
	Operations	Report from production manager indicating three more workers are needed	Three production jobs are advertised
	Office manager	Memo requesting a new photocopier	Use existing machine for one more year, as no money available for purchase
Database	Sales and marketing	Report showing one third of regular customers have not placed repeat orders this month	Find out why; then decide appropriate action, e.g. send letters to relevant customers
Spreadsheet	Finance	Profit and loss account showing profit has fallen by a half because of a fall in demand	Find out why; find out if other businesses are also affected; then decide appropriate action, e.g. adapt product specifications

Other examples of software applications are:

- **desktop publishing** – used for advanced page-layout techniques required in the production of high quality leaflets, magazines and booklets
- **graphics** – used for drawings, pictures and illustrations.

Questions 3

1 Information can be transmitted in various ways. Two of these are written and electronic.

  a Look carefully at the picture of the office. List four examples of written information which are shown there.

  b Look at the picture again. List three examples of electronic information shown in the picture.

  c Information can also be divided into internal and external information. From the picture of the office:

   (i) list three examples of internal information

   (ii) list four examples of external information

2 Businesses must decide what information is relevant to them.

CR

  a List four other things which they must consider about the information they receive.

  b The points shown in part **a** are the first part of the evaluation process. The second part involves looking at specific items such as **accounts**, **worker performance** and **production**.

  Use each bold word above as a heading and, under each heading, list the kinds of information which might be evaluated. The first item in the accounts list has been completed for you as an example.

Accounts	*comparison of profits between years*
Worker performance	
Production	

How do businesses produce goods and services?

Example: Making a CD

Input

People, e.g. singer, producer, engineer, musicians

Resources, e.g. recording equipment, recording studios, musical instruments

Input includes the raw materials, equipment and labour which are directly put into production or provision of a product or service.

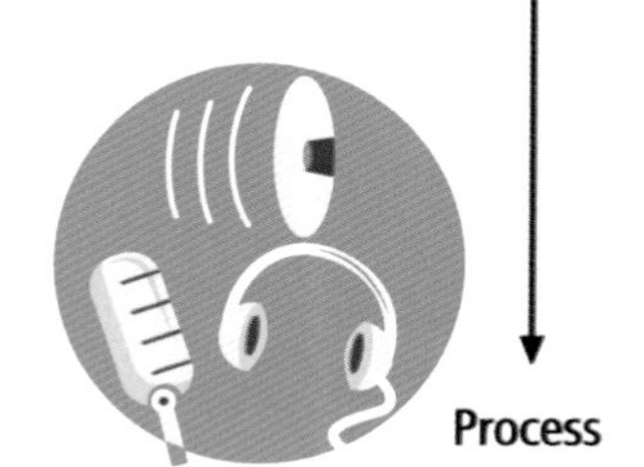

Process

The singer sings and the musicians play.

The producer supervises the singer and the musicians, as well as the recording process.

The engineer and the producer carry out the technical steps required to make, and perfect, the recording.

The process involves using the raw materials, equipment and labour to make the product or provide the service.

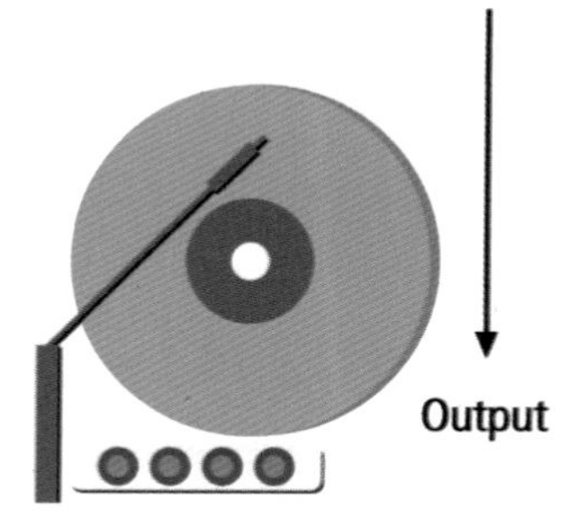

Output

The CDs are manufactured in bulk to be distributed to shops.

The output is the final product. In this example it is the CD.

How do products get to consumers?

Channels of distribution

Goods can be distributed from their place of production to the consumer in various ways and via different routes:

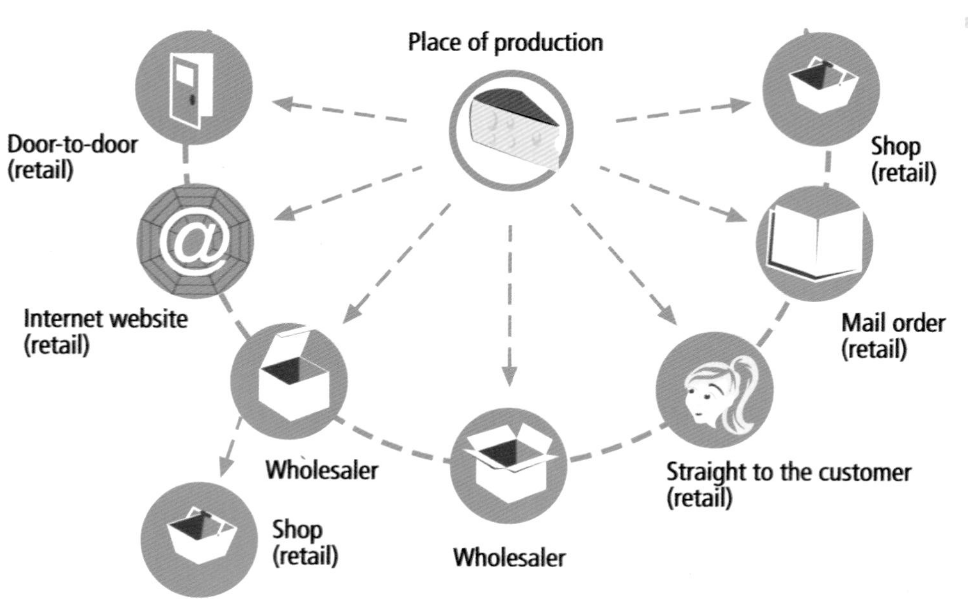

The channel chosen depends on a number of factors, including the nature of the product being sold. Hand-knitted jumpers and computers will probably be distributed in different ways from each other.

If the product is sold direct from the producer to the customer, then there is no 'middle man' taking a percentage of the sale price. For example, cheese sold by a dairy farmer at a farmer's market might be cheaper.

Alternatively, if he makes enough cheese, the farmer may sell it to a wholesaler, who might then sell direct to the customer (at a wholesale outlet) or to a retailer such as Sainsbury, who then sells the cheese to the customer.

Or, the farmer may sell direct to the retailer, who then sells the cheese to the customer.

Channel	*Customer*		*Producer*	
	Advantages	**Disadvantages**	**Advantages**	**Disadvantages**
Producer to customer	Cheaper goods and/or better quality because direct from producer	Less choice May have to collect goods, e.g. food from a farm	More profit Contact with customer, so better informed	Distracts producer from their main skill; a 'middle man' might market the goods better
Producer to wholesaler to customer	Cheaper goods because of wholesaler's economies of scale	Goods might be more expensive because wholesaler has a mark-up	Wholesaler takes responsibility for transport, packaging, etc.	Wholesaler takes some of the profit
Producer to wholesaler to retailer to customer	For example, corner shops: convenience, nearness to customers	Prices in the convenience store (e.g. corner shop) are usually higher	Wholesaler and retailer take responsibility for transport, distribution, etc.	Less profit because it is divided between more companies
Producer to retailer to customer	Cheaper than the chain which includes the wholesaler; specialist retailer can give helpful advice	Prices are higher because the retailer will have a mark-up in the same way that a wholesaler does	Retailers take on the marketing costs. This is why car manufacturers, for example, still sell through dealers	Less profit because they have to share with retailers

Production processes

- Job production involves a one-off project such as a film, specialist machinery or a unique house.
- Batch production is the process of making several identical (or very similar) products at once (e.g. casks of whisky and trays of seedlings).
- Flow process describes forms of production such as assembly lines. Car manufacturing is an example of this, where parts are added to the car one after the other by different people and/or technology. This is more of a non-stop process than batch production and involves larger numbers.

People versus machines

Use of technology (including automation) in primary and manufacturing industries

Advantages of technology include:

- increased output
- where workers are still involved, new technology can create better labour productivity (i.e. it allows workers to produce more)
- increased quality – less worker error
- greater variety – computer-aided machines are far more adaptable than older ones.

Disadvantages of technology include:

- cost of installation of equipment
- cost of training staff
- breakdowns and technical difficulties can stop workflow
- computer data can corrupt, causing inconvenience and/or cost
- may result in workers losing jobs.

Implications of technology for jobs

- Many jobs have been lost, especially in manufacturing where machines now do unskilled, repetitive tasks previously done by people.
- The demand for skilled workers has now increased.
- Skills are required to manage and control production – which cannot be done totally by machinery.
- Workers are increasingly expected to be multi-skilled.
- Governments and businesses have put money into education and training to increase the pool of appropriate, skilled labour.

Mechanisation This means workers are replaced by machines. However, workers still play a part in production. An example of this would be combine harvesters in farming, which need to be operated by people.

Full automation This is one step further than mechanisation, and involves replacing workers fully by machines. The machines are programmed to work alone with minimum supervision. Examples of this include car factories, in which most of the cars' components are assembled by robots.

Technology in service industries

In some service industries (e.g. banking and insurance) technology has also had a great impact on jobs. Cash-dispensing machines, debit cards, phone banking and internet banking have reduced visits to banks. However, service industries by their very nature still sometimes require people to provide direct links with customers. This is particularly true in the areas of marketing and customer complaints. Other jobs, such as a doctor's receptionist, still require the personal touch.

Stock control

CR

Stock control is an extremely important part of any business. It must be very accurate and closely monitored. If stock is lost or damaged, the business will lose money. There are several issues which have to be addressed.

- **Security** against internal and external theft is required. Security staff and/or cameras may be needed.
- **Record keeping** of amounts ordered, amounts received and amounts despatched must be very accurate. Computerisation of orders, stock cards and remittances helps here.
- **Accounting/costing** is very important in keeping track of costs. How much the stock cost helps determine whether suppliers are used again and how much profit needs to be added on.
- **Length of storing period** should not be too long. Most goods will deteriorate or go out of date if stored for a great length of time. Also stock ties up money, so most businesses do not like to keep too much.

Just-in-time (JIT) stock levels (where manufacturers order from suppliers as and when they need stock) are now proving popular. If JIT techniques are not used, ordering levels should be high enough to allow for delivery time, but low enough to ensure that stocks do not build up too much.

Advantages of JIT	*Disadvantages of JIT*
Up-to-date raw materials	Very dependent on suppliers for quality and punctuality
Undamaged supplies are vital	Production will be held up if supplies are late – no stock to fall back on
No over-stocking	Difficult to expand production at short notice due to lack of stock
No storage costs	
No money tied up in stock	

Quality assurance

Quality of products and of customer service are both very important. Targets should be set and monitored, and procedures should be set up to deal with areas in which quality is not meeting the targets. If product quality is poor, demand will fall, and so will profits.

In traditional businesses **quality control** and checking was the responsibility of one department or a small group of workers. It involved inspectors checking final products and scrapping them if they were substandard. However, waiting to the end of the production process caused a great deal of wastage.

Quality assurance was the next stage, where workers were organised in teams to ensure quality during and after the production process. These teams may be known as quality circles.

Total quality management is the most complete form of quality monitoring and control. It is also the newest method of quality control. Features include:

- involving customers in quality monitoring by asking how satisfied they are with the quality of product or service

- involving all workers in quality control, so that more people have responsibility for quality
- involving people working in teams to help each other achieve the highest possible quality. Each worker has equal responsibility for quality.

Just-in-time manufacturing techniques help to ensure high quality production because:

- businesses must ensure suppliers always provide undamaged goods, since the business has no stock to fall back on
- production at each stage must be perfect. If not, work will run out since there is no work-in-progress with which to continue production.

It can be risky but JIT means money is not tied up in stock unnecessarily. It is up to management to ensure highest quality production so that work does not run out.

Customer service

Customer service covers:

- the treatment of customers by sales staff on the phone, in the shop and at the checkout
- handling of queries and complaints
- customisation of letters to existing and potential customers advertising products and services
- after-sales service.

Sometimes checking the quality of customer service is carried out and/or monitored by a customer service department whose main job is to undertake and monitor customer services. Some businesses employ outside market research agencies to approach customers and ask them about their satisfaction with a particular company.

Improving customer service

To find out how to improve the service it gives its customers, a business needs to find out what its customers think. This can be done actively via market research (questionnaires, surveys, interviews, etc.). Loss of sales, especially from repeat customers, is probably a sign of dissatisfied customers, and poor customer service.

Customer service can generally be improved in a number of ways:

- getting things right, first time, every time
- improving the customer's experience of dealing with the business, whether this is modernising a shopfloor, having more operators to handle queries, or setting up a more user-friendly website
- communicating information accurately and efficiently
- ensuring orders are processed accurately and customers are invoiced correctly
- responding quickly and courteously to customer queries
- providing products on time and to the agreed price and quality
- acting in accordance with product guarantees and warranties
- responding efficiently and fairly to customer complaints and grievances.

Questions 4

1 a Explain what is meant by the term 'mechanisation'.

b In what way is 'automation' different from 'mechanisation'?

c In manufacturing industry, mechanisation and automation have caused many job losses.

(i) What kinds of jobs do you think this statement mainly refers to?

(ii) Give two advantages which automation brings to a manufacturer.

(iii) Give two examples of banking technology which have reduced the need for bank tellers.

d New technology has increased the demand for skilled workers. What are governments and businesses doing to increase the pool of skilled labour?

2 a Why is stock control a very important part of a business?

b Name and briefly explain four issues regarding stock control which must be addressed by businesses.

3 a Why is quality important to a business?

b Define the following terms, showing the differences between them:

(i) quality control

(ii) quality assurance

(iii) total quality management.

c (i) What is meant by just-in-time manufacturing techniques?

(ii) Give one advantage of using just-in-time manufacturing techniques.

(iii) Give one disadvantage of using just-in-time manufacturing techniques.

What are the challenges facing businesses?

Competition

Some examples of the type of competition which British businesses may face from both home and abroad are given below:

Competition from other UK businesses

- New ideas from other businesses
- Better quality of production
- Lower prices
- Better equipment/technology
- Existing, well-known products
- Competition from the internet/world wide web

- Lower wages/raw materials can lead to cheaper imports into Britain
- Some foreign governments subsidise their businesses, leading to cheaper imports into Britain (no longer allowed between EU countries)
- New ideas, better quality, lower prices

Rapidly expanding economies like China with relatively low prices and vast production levels are becoming major competitors.

CASE STUDY: THE MUSIC INDUSTRY

The process of making a CD is described on page 68. Businesses that produce CDs are now facing strong competition from the internet. More and more consumers are downloading music by file swapping rather than buying CDs. Until recently internet companies that facilitated this (often called 'fast track-based' companies) have been in direct opposition to large music companies.

The Recording Industry Association of America (RIAA) have sued the fast track-based companies and have sent hundreds of thousand of copyright infringement notices asking internet service providers and universities to stop file swappers.

However, there are signs that the music industry is considering other strategies. Some music executives are looking at ways to compete more directly with the file-swapping services. One idea is to offer a label-sponsored free service that would allow consumers to stream or download songs without charge. If customers wanted to keep the songs, burn CDs or move them from their computers, they then would have to pay.

Questions on case study

1 The music industry is now considering direct competition rather than legal action. Why do you think this is?
2 If file swapping is so popular, why do you think people still buy CDs?

Scarce resources

Businesses often work within the constraints of existing resources. Skilled labour, premises and land, equipment, finance and raw materials are relatively scarce – they are not infinite (i.e. they will not last forever).

Skilled labour

Some businesses find it difficult to find the appropriate skilled labour. Examples of scarce, skilled labour include engineers and computer experts. Since supply of this type of labour is very limited, the wages offered are sometimes very high. Small businesses might not be able to pay the high wages – which makes such resources very scarce indeed.

Land and premises

In some areas, such as city centres, there is a shortage of land and premises. This can lead to high rents and prices.

Specialist equipment

Specialist equipment can be very expensive. One example of this is hospital equipment.

Finance

Businesses often face cash flow problems. Small businesses tend to suffer most from this. Borrowing is often more difficult for a small business than for a large one.

Internal and external pressures

Internal pressures

Businesses face pressures from within. For example, it is advisable to keep workers as content as possible. This is often achieved by providing a good working environment, fair wages, reasonable promotion prospects and good training schemes. If not, the following can happen:

- poor quality production due to unmotivated staff

- poor industrial relations which can cause strikes, work-to-rule and picketing
- staff leave, and shortages of labour occur leading to a fall in production levels.

Other internal pressures which businesses might face can arise from:

- faulty equipment – which may make products which are poor quality, not produced on time and/or not up to the standard of competitors' products.
- not being able to keep costs down – faulty equipment causes high wastage levels and a high price of materials. Businesses are sometimes reluctant to pay the high costs of improvements to equipment and premises. However, it is advisable in the long run because staff will become unhappy in poor conditions, and production will suffer. This in turn can lead to less demand from customers and a fall in profits.
- shareholders who want profits to be as high as possible.

External pressures

Businesses are influenced by what happens in the world outside and they have to take these external factors into account. Examples of such external pressure businesses might face include:

- Suppliers can increase their charges, affecting the business's budgets and forecasts, or they may go out of business themselves (if they are a specialist supplier, this can cause major problems for the business).
- The government can change tax or the Bank of England can change interest rates, again affecting forecasts and profits, or the government can change regulations and legislation which the business must comply with. Legal and health issues such as safety of products (e.g. toys), anti-pollution requirements (e.g. in car exhaust systems), and copyright infringement can restrict the freedom of businesses to do what they like.
- Competitors can develop completely new products which dominate the market at short notice, eating into the business's market share (and therefore profit), or they could merge into a single larger business with better economies of scale, allowing it to reduce prices.
- Banks can increase interest rates on borrowings or refuse short-term loans to cover cash flow problems, which could cause such a cash-flow crisis that a business fails
- Environmental pressure groups can protest and raise certain issues in the media and damage the reputation of a business, or petition local authorities regarding intended developments, slowing down planned expansion.

External factors

CR

External factors are outside a business's control and can affect the business in negative and positive ways. Business must be able to react to external factors, known as PEST factors:

- Political
- Economic
- Socio-cultural
- Technological.

Businesses usually have to make decisions based not only on the external factors, but on internal factors too, and compromises often have to be made.

Political

Governments can affect businesses directly through changes to legislation (e.g. employment, environment), regulations (e.g. international trade rules, competition, consumer protection), and taxation (corporate tax rates). The different beliefs of political parties means they act differently when in power. Traditionally, Conservative governments are more likely to implement lower taxes thus encouraging enterprise and capitalism. Labour governments have tended to increase taxes in order to support public/social services and the welfare state. Government policies and priorities determine the amount of funding available for certain sectors – for example, the decision to go to war necessarily diverts money from other areas, and potentially leads to tax rates being increased to cover additional costs.

Economic

The state of the national and global economy also affects business. If an economy is in **recession**, there is not much new business activity, less investment, and consumers are less likely to spend, especially on non-essential items. In a period of high unemployment, businesses will often reduce wage rates, knowing that the need for paid employment is such that workers will accept lower wages. In a period of high **inflation**, goods and services not only cost more, but the actual purchasing power of currency decreases, so its value is less.

Recession In a recession, the economy slows down until a recovery when activity begins to improve again.

Inflation Inflation is the general continuous increase in the price of goods and services that is not matched by an increase in production over a period of time. Moderate inflation of 2–3% per year is good, indicating manageable growth in the economy. Zero inflation means the economy is flat (not growing). A high inflation rate means costs are out of control.

Socio-cultural

Environmental and health issues are becoming more and more important in the decision making of many businesses. BAA – the owner of Heathrow airport – wants to build another terminal. This is very important for the expansion of its business. At present it is finding it difficult to cope with the number of planes and passengers that use its facilities. However, this step is proving very unpopular with environmentalists and campaigners who argue that planes pollute the atmosphere and contribute to global warming. BAA, therefore, has to try and reach a compromise between progress for customers and an increase in its profits, while considering the implications for the environment. Government intervention may be required to solve the dispute.

Manufacturers and retailers of food also face criticism regarding the unhealthy content of many processed foods. Processed foods became popular because they saved busy people time when preparing meals.

However, the high sugar, fat and salt content of many of these foods is being criticised and large food retailers like Tesco and Marks & Spencer are beginning to take notice. Like BAA, these retailers must balance profit making with outside influences.

Technology

The use of technology such as robots, computers and highly automated production lines, has helped to improve the quality and quantity of goods and services produced. However, it has also meant the loss of jobs, as robots and computers have meant that fewer workers were required in some industries.

Questions 5

1 Popudrinks Ltd is a large soft drinks manufacturer. The factory, although working at full capacity, is becoming run-down. Falling plaster injured a worker recently and faulty equipment nearly caused another accident shortly afterwards. Employees are becoming worried and restless.

- **a** Describe three types of staff responses which might soon occur if these problems are not resolved.
- **b** (i) Why do you think the management of Popudrinks Ltd have been reluctant to make the necessary improvements?
  - (ii) Why do you think these improvements are necessary?
- **c** There are two main types of pressures faced by businesses – internal and external. Which one of these terms describes the pressures faced by Popudrinks Ltd?

2 A large construction business has won the contract to build an eight-lane motorway through attractive countryside. The project will take 4 years to build and will pass near some villages and a town.

- **a** Describe the internal pressures which the business might face.
- **b** The business will also face external pressures. List three socio-cultural issues that the business may face.

CHAPTER 4
HOW ARE BUSINESSES MANAGED?

What are the key decisions that businesses make?

Key decisions

Businesses must make decisions about the following issues:

- what to produce
- what to charge
- whom to employ
- where to produce
- whether to conduct market research
- the balance of human labour and machines used in production
- whether the firm should grow
- the marketing mix
- the combination of the factors of production.

Questions, questions…

What to produce

Depending on the type of business, this decision will be made by different people. In a sole trader business, it will be made by the owner. In a small, new business this decision will be made by the entrepreneur who starts up the business. In a large business, it will be decided by senior managers. In a partnership it will be decided by partners.

Factors which help in making the decision about what to produce include:

- the managers' and/or entrepreneur's own ideas of 'gaps in the market'
- asking the public what they think about proposed goods and services through market research
- looking at the products of competitors and deciding whether the same products could be made at a lower cost, of better quality, or in a better version

- looking at resources available and deciding whether the product could be made locally or abroad.

Businesses might use a range of market research methods to find out if the public will buy the proposed product, such as:

- field research – questionnaires and surveys (face to face, telephone, postal, online), focus groups, market testing
- desk research – analysing competitors' products.

See pages 23–25 for more information about market research methods.

What to charge

When the type of product or service is decided, its price must also be considered. Important factors include the following:

- price of competitors' products
- quality of the product
- cost of materials and labour required to make it
- required profit margin
- how much the business thinks customers will be prepared to pay.

In general, when price is increased sales fall; and when price is decreased sales rise. However, the market intended for the product may affect this. If a product is to be marketed as a luxury, for example, it might sell better if it is priced accordingly. Certain up-market perfumes are priced in this way. They are highly priced in order to maintain an image – the price does not necessarily reflect the cost of making them. On the other hand, if the product is mass-produced and is aimed at the lower end of the market, a lower price should increase sales.

Whom to employ

Factors to consider include the following:

- funds available: a small business might not be able to afford many staff
- type of product: specialist staff might be a necessity for some products – even in a very small business (e.g. a pharmacist in a chemist shop)
- availability of appropriate staff: a business might have to train its own staff, which has time and cost implications
- duties required, and level of training –for example, a legal secretary or medical secretary need extra training.

Where to produce

This can depend on the following:

- necessity for raw materials: some raw materials (such as certain minerals) can only be found abroad. If this is the case, it might be more efficient to produce the goods abroad
- requirements for low-cost labour: there is a tendency for more and more British businesses to contract out work to factories in developing countries. The products can be made abroad and transported to Britain for a lower price than it would cost to make them here
- low-cost premises and rent: assisted areas can be attractive to businesses because of the subsidies and low rents which are available

- availability of appropriate premises and land: many retailers are acquiring land out of towns in order to build large superstores and spacious parking facilities.

See pages 46–48 for more information about factors affecting location of industry.

Market research

It has been argued that, until recently, British businesses produced goods first and sought people's opinions on their products second, or not at all. People were expected to be happy with what they were given.

Nowadays, the importance of market research is recognised, and managers must decide:

- whether or not to use market research
- what type to use – field research or desk research
- what questions to ask potential customers
- whether to do the market research themselves, or whether to employ an outside agency, e.g. MORI.

Market research, if done correctly, will give managers a better idea of what people want and how much they would be prepared to pay. If prices are too high, some goods will not sell at all. Some products (e.g. designer clothes) are deliberately priced highly to emphasise the idea of status or luxury.

Method	*Advantages*	*Disadvantages*
Face to face interview	Interviewer can seek clarification if answers are confusing or inconsistent – better quality information	Training of interviewers can be costly Interviews can be time consuming
Telephone survey	Lots of people can be questioned quite quickly Immediate responses	Cost of training interviewers Resentment towards interviewers because phone calls are seen as intrusive
Focus group	Opportunity for wide-ranging responses	Can be difficult to analyse the information obtained
Postal survey	Inexpensive to produce and to analyse	Low response rates Simplicity of questions means that responses will be within limited scope
Online survey	Inexpensive to produce and to analyse	Low response rates Simplicity of questions means that responses will be within limited scope
Product testing	Information is gained about the actual product (not about the idea of the product)	Can be difficult to analyse the information obtained
Desk research	Inexpensive Wide range of sources can be researched	Data is also available to competitors Data may be out of date

People versus machines

Managers must decide which combination of people and machines is suitable for their business. Important terms to understand are **capital intensive** and **labour intensive**.

Capital Capital refers to the financial costs of equipment used to produce and distribute goods and services.

Labour Labour refers to the human workers required for the production and distribution of goods and services.

Capital intensive

- Capital intensive production means that technology and other equipment are used in a larger proportion than human workers and cost more than labour.
- This type of production is likely to be used in flow production, in industries such as car assembly factories, bottling plants and processed food production, all of which are highly automated.

Labour intensive

- Labour intensive production means that labour is used in a larger proportion than capital and costs more than the capital used.
- This type of production is likely to be used in job production or in production that requires individual or small-scale processes.

Advantages and disadvantages of capital and labour intensive processes

Capital intensive processes	
Advantages	**Disadvantages**
Large scale production is possible, leading to economies of scale	Breakdowns can occur
Products should be identical so easier to maintain same level of quality	It can be costly to increase or decrease scale of production
Speed of production is much quicker than that produced by labour	Very high costs are involved in the purchase, maintenance and replacement of the technology

Labour intensive proceses	
Advantages	**Disadvantages**
Flexibility in capacity through overtime, etc.	Large numbers of workers are very costly and unlike technology they do not provide the same economies of scale
Labour provides the personal touch	Recruitment of staff is difficult in some industries
Where it is important that products are individual, labour is required to produce them	Human error

Decisions on the combination of capital and labour to be used will depend on:

- the type of product or service which is being produced
- the type of jobs done, e.g. a computer may replace some machinists in a factory. Replacing a receptionist is less likely. The personal touch is still important in the reception area of a business
- the availability of technology to do the job
- the availability of people to do the job
- relative costs of people versus technology.

Industries where products and services can be improved through technology

- Large scale production of items like cars, bottling of drinks, are improved by using technology because more can be produced; the time of production is much quicker; and goods are identical to each other (on the whole) which allows for better quality control.
- Health services – equipment such as scanners and technology used in radiography and surgery can give doctors information that would otherwise be very difficult to obtain.
- Communication services such as TV, radio and telephone systems have been improved through the use of satellites, computerisation and other technology. The range of TV and radio services has increased worldwide; the speed at which information can be sent is increasing all the time.

Whether the firm should grow

When a business grows this usually means an increase in all or some of the following:

- size of premises
- amount of funds available
- amount of workers available
- amount of equipment, technology, vehicles, that it can use
- the number, and variety, of products and services that it can produce.

In theory, the increased capacity of these areas will allow the firm to sell more products for the following reasons.

- Bigger premises allows the firm to handle and process (and therefore sell) more products, whether that means producing them, storing them, distributing them, or all three.
- The increase in available funds allows the company to invest in better equipment, buy more raw materials, etc., and the firm can use these resources to make and sell more products.
- More workers should increase production, and also sales (however, when firms grow through mergers, this often results in staff cuts).
- More equipment and technology should increase production capacity, and therefore increase **sales volume**. It can also reduce the cost per unit produced, which can lower the sales price; this may increase **sales revenue** and profit.
- By increasing the variety and number of products that it can produce, a firm increases the variety and number it can sell.

However, growth does not automatically lead to increased sales or increased profits. Management must decide, through market research and knowledge of the market generally:

- if demand warrants increased production
- whether the products or services lend themselves to mass production and growth. Some high quality and individualised products like jewellery at the top end of the market, do not. Profits are increased by raising price, not producing more.
- whether growth is the best way to compete with other businesses.

Sales volume The number of units sold.

Sales revenue The total money received by the firm from the units sold.

Marketing mix

An important element of marketing is known as the marketing mix, or 4 Ps, which are: Product, Price, Promotion and Place.

It is very important that businesses give serious attention to the following:

- designing and developing a **product** (see page 25 for an explanation of prototype)
- getting the **price** right
- making sure customers know about the product through **promotion**
- making sure the product is on sale in the correct **place**.

The marketing mix: Product

Hint

The term 'product' is used in this context even if a service is being produced.

The product (including service) is the most important part of the marketing mix. There is little point in making sure the other three Ps are correct if the product has major problems, e.g. it is poor quality or there is no market for it. A business should make the following decisions about its products:

- what product (or range of products) the business will sell. Before production begins, a business must be sure that there is a market for its product. This will determine what product is made.
- what the product will be called: the name of the product should be relevant to its purpose and easy to pronounce and to remember.
- how the product should be packaged: factors affecting packaging include:
  - packaging has a practical use as it protects the product(s) inside it (e.g. canned foods)
  - transport and storage – bottles, for example, should have flat bottoms to keep them stable on shelves
  - packaging should include information about its contents
  - its colour and shape name can attract customers

    - in some cases, the brand (either of the product itself or the business) will be prominent
    - packaging can give the correct quality signals, e.g. up-market perfume.
    - depending on the target market, environmental issues may be important, for example, is the packaging made of recycled or recyclable materials?
- what the product life cycle will be.

The marketing mix: Price

Price is another very important part of the marketing mix. The three key elements that must be considered about 'price' by a business are:

- what competitors are charging for their products
- how price can promote a product and/or increase its sales
- what the price needs to cover.

Competitors' prices

Undercutting competitors' prices would get sales, but by how much depends on the product. Where image is important, a product which is much less expensive than competitors' prices might give the wrong image, e.g. 'cheap and nasty'. If the price is too much above those of competitors, however, customers might not buy. The business must strike a balance in its pricing policy.

Different pricing strategies

Destroyer pricing

Destroyer pricing is used when businesses deliberately undercut their competitors with low prices in order to destroy the competition altogether. It is also known as predator pricing. It can often mean that prices are set below cost for a certain time. Large businesses can often afford this more than small ones. For example, the very low price of product A increases demand for it and destroys demand for competition product B; once B is eliminated, the price of product A can be raised again.

Penetration pricing

Penetration pricing is used with new products, to encourage sales at the launch of the product to attract sales, before customer loyalty is built up. When that has occurred and the product established, the price can then be raised.

Skimming

Skimming involves setting a high price initially before lowering it. Skimming occurs in high fashion, when products are produced in small numbers. The products are often of high quality and give the purchaser an up-market image. It also occurs with new technology, when the first products are bought by enthusiasts who are willing to pay a high price in order to be one of the first people to own the product. Later on, the goods are mass produced (sometimes of lower quality) and the price is much lower.

Cost-plus

The cost-plus pricing strategy involves adding a percentage on to the cost price to arrive at the selling price. This percentage is also known as the mark-up.

What the price needs to cover

Businesses often set prices according to what they believe the market can bear. For example, products are sometimes priced differently according to the country in which they are sold. Prices of the same brand of trainers tend to be much more expensive in Britain than in the USA.

In the long term, price must exceed costs, and pricing strategies such as penetration and destroyer pricing – which might not cover costs – only last for limited periods until their desired effects are achieved, whether that is to give sales a temporary boost or to destroy the competition.

When to use a particular pricing strategy

Firms must decide which is the best strategy for them at a particular time.

Destroyer pricing

- Although skimming and penetration pricing are normally used when introducing new products, destroyer pricing can be used for established products too.
- An example of destroyer pricing occurred in the 1990s when the *Times* newspaper reduced its price; other competitors followed, and the *Today* newspaper went out of business in 1995.
- It is often carried out by large, well established firms who can afford the cut in price for a short period of time.

Penetration pricing

- In theory, customers will buy more as a result of reduced prices.
- A firm is trying to bring a new product on to the market. The product can be mass produced, making unit costs low. A long life cycle is predicted for the new product, e.g. food products like KitKat.
- The firm has to be able to afford the initial low price. This is why it would use penetration pricing with a product that it thinks will last for a long time, because it expects to cover the initial costs by achieving long-term sales in the future. It is also likely to be easier for a large, established firm to do this – but not always.

Skimming

- In theory, customers respond more to the uniqueness or quality of the product than the price, and so are prepared to pay a high price.
- The life cycle of the product is expected to be relatively short, e.g. versions of computer games. The product is heavily promoted and there are relatively few competitors.
- Well established firms like Microsoft, Apple or Sony who produce computers, electronic games, TV products, etc. often charge high prices at the beginning of some products' lives. This covers the high initial cost of development and attracts customers who want to be the first owners of a new product. The first large plasma TV screens were an example of this type of product.

The marketing mix: Promotion

Promotion is what businesses do to make customers aware of their products and services and encourage them to buy. By promoting their products, businesses:

- inform the market about new products
- remind the market of existing products
- persuade the market to buy the products.

Promotion includes different sorts of 'deals' such as money-off, discount vouchers, better value offers, free gifts, competitions and tastings. Such sales promotions aim to give a short-term boost to sales. Promotion also includes advertising and the use of press releases and public or media relations.

Businesses must make decisions about these aspects of promotion:

- whether the product should promoted/advertised, and if so, how
- what the cost of promotion/advertising will be
- the best way to target the market
- whether the business should advertise by itself or use an outside agency.

Methods of promotion

Money-off coupons

These can be obtained from the packaging of products; they can be cut out of newspapers; or they can come straight from suppliers. They enable customers to buy more products and services for a reduced price. This encourages people to buy the products in the first place.

Competitions

Customers can enter competitions that are related to products and services. This encourages them to buy the product or service first.

Free gifts

A free gift can be given with a product. Many cosmetic firms use this method, e.g. Clinique's 'bonus time'. Clinique's 'bonus time' usually occurs before or after busy times like summer holidays, Christmas, etc. and is used to keep sales up before or after these peak buying times. Customers usually have to buy two or more products before they qualify for the free gift.

Two for the price of one

Promotions like 'buy one get one free' offer two items for the price of one – one costs 75p but two can be bought for £1, giving an apparent 'saving' of 50p. However, the customer has been encouraged to pay more overall and to buy more products.

Loyalty cards

Loyalty cards have become extremely popular in recent years. Retailers like Tesco and Asda offer them to their customers. Customers use these cards when buying products and services, and earn points for their purchases. This encourages them to remain loyal to certain retailers, and to buy the bulk of their purchases there.

Loyalty cards

Loyalty cards not only encourage shoppers to be loyal to a particular company, but they also provide information about the shopping habits of customers that is very valuable to the company. When the customer first obtains the loyalty card they provide personal information, such as their age, address, occupation, etc. So when they buy goods, the firm can see what they buy, when they buy, and can identify trends for particular age groups, etc.

Hint

The terms 'promotion' and 'advertising' are very closely linked. Advertising tends to mean giving information about a product via media like newspapers, posters, TV, internet, etc. Promotion tends to mean 'deals' such as three for two, or money–off vouchers, etc. However, promotion is a form of advertising and advertising is a form of promotion, so it can be difficult to separate them!

Advertising

Not all businesses decide to advertise, but if they do, their reasons are:

- to let customers know the product is there
- to tell them what it is and what it does
- to try to persuade customers to buy the product
- to tell them the ways in which their product is better than existing products.

Types of advertising include:

- TV
- radio
- cinema
- leaflets
- press releases
- internet
- newspapers
- magazines
- books
- billboards
- sky writing
- posters.

Public relations and media releases

Large companies use press releases to keep people up to date about their products and services. These help promote the company and keep it in the public eye, but they can also serve to allay fears and criticisms about their activities, for example, Tesco's continued and rapid expansion policy. Many of these companies publish such media releases on their own websites.

Internet research

Visit the websites of some large companies such as Tesco, Unilever and Marks & Spencer, and look at some of their press releases. In what ways do you think these press releases promote the companies? Write short notes on this.

Links to these sites and other websites relating to Standard Grade Business Management can be found at: **www.leckieandleckie.co.uk** by clicking on the Learning Lab button and navigating to the Standard Grade Business Management Course Notes page.

LECKIE&LECKIE Learning Lab

Deciding on types of promotion and advertising

CR

Large companies often have large budgets but even they have to advertise cost-effectively. It would be pointless to spend thousands of pounds on a TV advertisement for a job vacancy, for example, when this could be done for much less in a newspaper. They will have to consider what kind of people they want to target.

Deciding on the best way to target the market

Businesses should find out what their sector of the market is e.g. old, young, female, male, etc. This can be discovered through market research. Once discovered, the adverts and medium used (e.g. TV, internet) should be suitable for targeting these people. For example, SAGA products and services are aimed at the over 50s. They advertise in products that are bought by that age group such as *Yours Magazine*.

Deciding on whether the business should advertise by itself or use an outside agency

The following should be considered:

- Does the business have its own marketing or publicity department?
- Can its own publicity department do the work, or should an outside agency be brought in for certain projects?
- Will advertising be very costly? Even if it is, will it be worth it in terms of increased sales?
- The agency is likely to have better contacts and specialised staff in the world of advertising.
- Using an agency allows the business to concentrate on production and selling.

The marketing mix: Place

The three main issues that must be addressed when choosing the right 'place' in which to make products or services are:

- deciding what the right place is
- deciding on the best distribution method
- getting the product to the right place at the right time

Deciding what the right place is

The 'right place' is affected by:

- technology – traditionally, a customer collected their money over a counter at a bank, whereas today, technology enables them to collect money at a bank auto-teller or a cashpoint at a supermarket
- the type of product – for example, frozen goods must be purchased from a shop or vehicle which has freezer facilities
- where the customer is – more customers buy goods and services from home, using the internet. Even traditional companies like Marks & Spencer sell their products online.

Deciding the best distribution method

CR

Main distribution methods are:

- manufacturer to retailer to customer
- manufacturer to wholesaler to retailer to customer
- manufacturer to customer
- manufacturer to wholesaler to customer.

Infrastructure such as road, rail, and air terminals also plays an important part in distribution. Costs of different transport systems also play a major part in deciding the best method of getting the product to the right place.

Getting the product to the right place at the right time is also important. This will be determined partly by cost, the location of the business, infrastructure and distribution channels, as well as the type of product, the type and size of the market, and the competition.

The product life cycle

The product life cycle measures the stages of a product from development to replacement or withdrawal from sale. These six stages are:

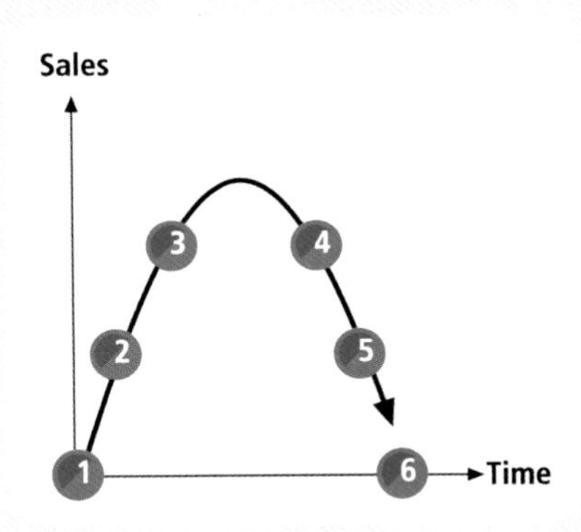

1 development
2 growth
3 maturity (which businesses try to extend)
4 saturation
5 decline
6 replacement or withdrawal.

The way the product is priced and promoted can vary at different stages of the life cycle.

Extension strategies

The marketing mix can be changed to inject new life into a product by:

- changing or modifying the product
- altering the distribution pattern
- changing the price
- using a promotional campaign.

This can delay stage 6 (the replacement or withdrawal stage) for some time.

CASE STUDY: KITKAT CHUNKY

KitKat, a brand leader manufactured by Nestlé, is an example of a product that was modified. The range that included the traditional two and four finger bars (which had been around for a long time) was revitalised by the launch of a new chunky bar. This new bar was targeted at the 18–25 age group, and market research showed that this age group was attracted to a single chunky finger. Researchers also looked at types of packaging that this group most admired. It was important that the new product be noticed by the public quickly, so its launch had to be supported by well targeted advertising and promotional activities. These included: TV adverts, phone site campaign, advertising targeted at 18–25 year olds, PR activities through TV and press, attractive dump-bins in stores and posters.

The launch in 1999 was very successful. Over 50 million bars were dispatched within the first few weeks of the launch. Other age groups became interested in the new and existing bars so the launch of the new product had little negative impact on other age groups. The life of KitKat was successfully extended.

Questions on case study

1. State one reason why you think Nestlé introduced the new Chunky bar in order to extend the life of KitKat.
2. State two things that were researched by Nestlé
3. Do you think the increased sales of the range as a whole was due only to the 18–25 age group? Give reasons for your answer.
4. At what stage (of a possible six) in the life cycle, do think the life of KitKat was extended?

Branding

CR

Branding is an important part of promotion. Products are given a name or brand to make people buy them, as much for the brand as for the product itself. Certain brands of sportswear, soft drinks and foodstuffs have this kind of image. Producers must decide what image they want their products to have – up-market and expensive or affordable and plentiful. This helps determine the pricing and distribution decisions. As can be seen, brand and image often go together.

Brand names can be widened to cover other unrelated products. For example, Virgin was originally a record shop. Now, however, there are many Virgin products and services, including travel.

Branding is important because:

- it builds up customer loyalty
- it conveys a message to customers. For example a brand can be intended to stand for quality (Gucci), for youth (Topshop), for healthy and environmentally friendly living (Innocent drinks). These attract the relevant customers to the business.
- it can help build a good reputation that will encourage suppliers and financial providers. A well known brand is more likely to attract financial backing and the goodwill of suppliers than a less well known brand.

The main aim of branding is to increase sales. By building up loyalty, by creating particular markets, and by building a good reputation, it is hoped that a brand will beat competitors and will encourage an extended life cycle.

Company brand versus product brand

Some products sell because of their **own** brand names. For example, people might buy a KitKat because of the product's name, not because of the name of the producer.

However, some items like Nike products sell better because of the **producer's** name rather than the name of an individual product.

Try to think of three products that sell because of their own brand names, and three that sell because of the makers' name.

Possible answers include: Smarties, Shockwaves styling mousse and iPod (product brands), and Chanel, Gucci and McDonald's (producer brands). Did you think of others?

The combination of the factors of production

CR

The four factors of production are land, labour, capital and enterprise. Enterprise is usually provided by the owner and/or managers of a business. The owner/managers then have to decide how best to combine the other three factors of production. The type of product/service that is produced can affect the combination of the factors of production which management decide to use. The following examples show how factors may be combined differently for different types of business.

Example 1

The manager has two options. Option 1 is to combine capital (computer) and labour (receptionist). Option 2 is to choose either capital or labour. Since it is advisable to have a person in the reception area who can perform some administration tasks using the computer, the better choice is the combination of computer and receptionist (option 1).

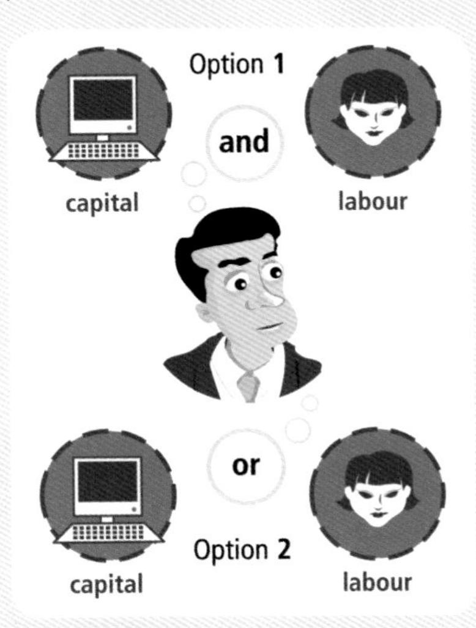

Example 2

The manager of a factory used for flow production, e.g. a car assembly plant, will need lots of land for the factory. Land and capital are then likely to be combined almost equally, since a car assembly plant also requires large amounts of technology and robotics.

large factory using a lot of land

Example 3

The manager of a capital intensive business, such as a highly computerised bank, would find a high-rise building suitable. Therefore, more capital than land is required in this example.

high rise building needing less land

Internet research

Visit the website of the FT 100. Choose one of the companies in the case study list, and take notes of some of the business decisions it has made.

Links to this site and other websites relating to Standard Grade Business Management can be found at: **www.leckieandleckie.co.uk** by clicking on the Learning Lab button and navigating to the Standard Grade Business Management Course Notes page.

Questions 1

1. Market research is now seen as an important tool for managers. After management decides to use market research, what three choices regarding market research are they then likely to make? **DM**
2. Managers also have to decide what combination of machines and people they want to employ. Describe three factors which will influence their decision. **DM**
3. Name three factors which must be considered when a business is deciding whether or not to expand its operations. **DM**

What influences decisions?

A car manufacturer will have to consider many factors if it decides to produce a completely new model of car.

Manufacturer's needs
- low costs
- high profits
- high demand

Customer needs
- good-looking car
- reliability
- good price
- low running cost
- safety, e.g. air bags

Economic climate
- interest rates for borrowing
- employment levels
- taxation levels
- value of pound sterling

Legal requirements
- exhaust system which meets anti-pollution requirements
- seat belts

Competition
- prices
- models

Social and environmental issues
- condition of infrastructure, i.e. roads
- peer pressure/perception
- living standards of potential customers
- environmental issues like cutting CO_2 emissions; new types of fuel, e.g. electric cars

Political environment
- attitudes to small cars and motorway tolls
- policies regarding foreign competition

Refer back to pages 40 and 75–77 for more information on external pressures that affect the decisions made by a business.

Legal, social, economic and political environment

The car manufacturer in the example above has to balance its needs for low costs, high profits and high demand from customers against the legal requirements of the government. It cannot leave out seat belts in order to cut costs (and lower prices) because that would not be legal.

There is no point in making luxury cars in a social environment where living standards are not very high, or in an economic climate where the cost of borrowing is very high. Luxury cars require large loans for many people.

The cost of production and the prices of competitors have to be considered. When a new car is produced, it should not be much more expensive than the equivalent models of competitors. On the other hand, it should not be so poorly made, or so ugly, that customers will not buy it!

The cost of driving also has to be considered. If a car is economical to run and maintain, this will help overcome other political and economic considerations such as having to pay tolls on motorways, bridges and car parking. This will make it attractive to customers.

Other economic factors

When interest rates are low, customers are more able to obtain and afford loans to buy a car. When interest rates are high, it is harder for customers to get loans, and running costs become more important. Any car which has low running costs will be particularly attractive during a period of high interest rates.

Taxation levels also affect people's ability and willingness to buy a new car. High income tax will cut people's spending power. High road tax and VAT will add to the running costs of cars which might lower the demand for new cars.

The value of the pound sterling in comparison with the currencies of other countries makes imported cars more (or less) expensive.

Employment levels generally affect the spending power in the whole country. When there is high unemployment, people might prefer to buy cheaper second-hand cars than more expensive new ones. This could make the manufacturer decide to postpone, or cancel, plans to produce a new model.

Sometimes governments give subsidies to car manufacturers. If this is done by foreign governments to their own companies, it makes British cars less competitive. This is a political and economic issue. Within the EU, however, governments are not allowed to subsidise their own industries.

The manufacturer has to consider and balance all the other factors listed on page 92, and decide which factors are most important. These will influence the type of car which is finally produced.

All types of businesses have to consider these factors.

Other legal considerations

Legal requirements affect management decisions. As well as those described elsewhere, managers must consider these factors.

- When recruiting for staff, managers must remember that candidates for the job cannot be discriminated against on the grounds of race or sex – the Race Relations Act 1976 and the Sex Discrimination Act 1975 make this illegal.
- When selling products, managers must comply with the Trade Descriptions Act 1968 which states that it is illegal to describe goods wrongly.

Other environmental issues

There are many environmental and health issues that affect companies. Some of those that are much mentioned in the media now are:

- healthy eating
- global warming and sustainable development
- fair trade.

Some food retailers are responding to these issues. Marks & Spencer advertise that they now put less salt into their food, and many large retailers are trying to discourage use of plastic bags. Fair trade goods are also now more commonly available.

CASE STUDY: CORKS VERSUS SCREW TOPS ON WINE BOTTLES

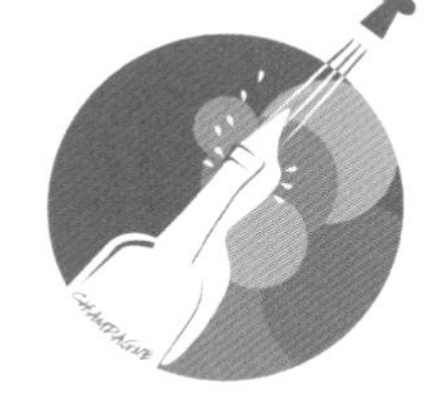

In 2002 the World Wildlife Fund launched a campaign to encourage people to choose wine and champagne with genuine cork stoppers rather than screw tops and plastic tops – with the aim of protecting the world's rarest big cat, the Iberian lynx.

The higher demand for non-cork-bottled alcohol has led to a fall in demand for real cork. Strangely, this has threatened the viability of cork forests in Spain and Portugal, because foresters are tempted to replace the cork forests with more profitable and less environmentally forms of agriculture ... and this is threatening the security of the endangered Iberian lynx which lives in the cork forests.

According to WWF, the cork forests are home to a rich variety of endangered wildlife, and cork extraction is one of the most environmentally friendly harvesting processes in the world, because trees are not actually cut down, and they are carefully maintained.

Competition from screw tops is threatening jobs as well as cork forests and the animals that live there. It has been known for a long time, however, that cork has properties that can sometimes damage wine. But manufacturers in Portugal, which accounts for more than 60 per cent of global trade, claim to have minimised this through improvements in manufacture.

Questions on case study

1 State two reasons why using corks is said to be environmentally friendly.

2 **a** What is threatening cork production?

b (i) Name one disadvantage of using cork in wine bottles

(ii) How can this disadvantage be overcome?

3 Which country accounts for most of the world's cork production?

Questions 2

1 **a** The management of a large car manufacturing company decides to produce a new model of car. They must first consider:

(i) the customers' needs

(ii) their own needs

(iii) competition from other businesses.

Copy and complete the following table by listing what you think the needs of each group will be. Two examples have been completed for you.

Customers' needs	*Manufacturer's needs*	*Competition from other businesses*
	low costs	cheaper prices

b The manufacturer must also consider social and legal issues. State and explain two examples of each. 

c (i) Name two economic factors affecting customers' buying power. 

(ii) Explain how these economic factors will affect the car manufacturer's decision about what type of car to make. DM

(iii) How can an economic and political decision such as putting toll charges on British motorways affect the type of car which a business decides to make? DM

2 Zigzag Trading Company employs 30 workers. It advertises for a secretary to the Sales Manager. The three applicants pictured are short-listed. The three candidates have similar academic qualifications and work experience. The management must treat the three applicants fairly, and employ one of them on merit. By law, there must be no unfair discrimination.

a Describe three examples of legislation which the management of Zigzag Trading Company must remember when considering the three applicants.

b The successful candidate is given a contract of employment to sign. Why do you think the management asked for this to be done?

Sankha Nahar

Frances O'Neill

Roy Mearns

What aids decision making?

Information helps decision making

Managers use information when they make decisions. This information can come from a range of sources (company sales figures, stock market figures, newspaper articles, market research, etc.), but wherever it comes from, it needs to be up to date and accurate. A manager who makes a decision based on a 2-year old survey may decide to produce a product that their competition launched successfully the previous year!

Types of information

Remember that information is either **internal** (found in sales reports, staff appraisals and final accounts) or **external** (found in newspapers, government statistics and on the internet).

Information is also **primary** or **secondary**. Primary information is gathered by an organisation, usually for a specific purpose – to get feedback from customers about a new product or as market research about ways to improve customer service. Secondary information is gathered from published sources outside the organisation and although it may have been published for one purpose, the organisation may use the collected information for a different purpose.

See pages 62–64 for more details on different types and sources of information, and pages 101–102 for more details on methods of communicating information.

Range of information used in decision making

CR

Managers often use graphs and charts to help them make decisions. A sales chart for 6 months is shown on page 96, and beside it are the sales targets for the same period. These are both examples of primary **and** internal information.

The sales chart shows actual sales while the sales target sheet shows what managers had aimed for each month.

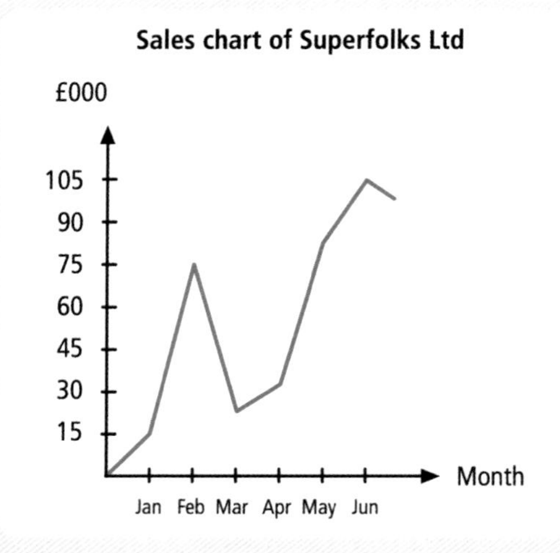

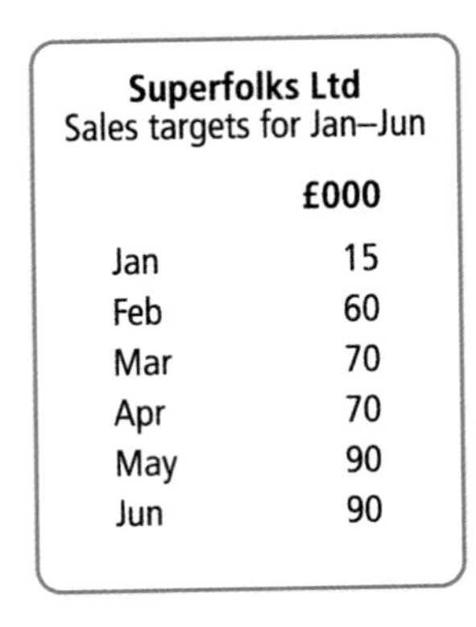

Superfolks Ltd
Sales targets for Jan–Jun

	£000
Jan	15
Feb	60
Mar	70
Apr	70
May	90
Jun	90

Management will look at the sales chart and the sales target sheet to see whether or not sales targets had been achieved each month. However, this information does not tell managers why sales were very bad in some months and very good in others. They would have to get that information from elsewhere, for example:

- information about the absences of salespeople in March and April could be found in staff records.
- information about the results of individual salespeople could be obtained from the sales manager.
- managers could decide whether the March and April targets were realistic by looking at the sales charts of previous years. If sales are always very low during these months, then the targets should be changed.

If the management of Superfolks wanted to compare these figures with those of public limited companies, they could access their accounts. This would be an example of secondary and external information.

Decision making model

Making decisions about the sales chart information could follow a model like the one shown below.

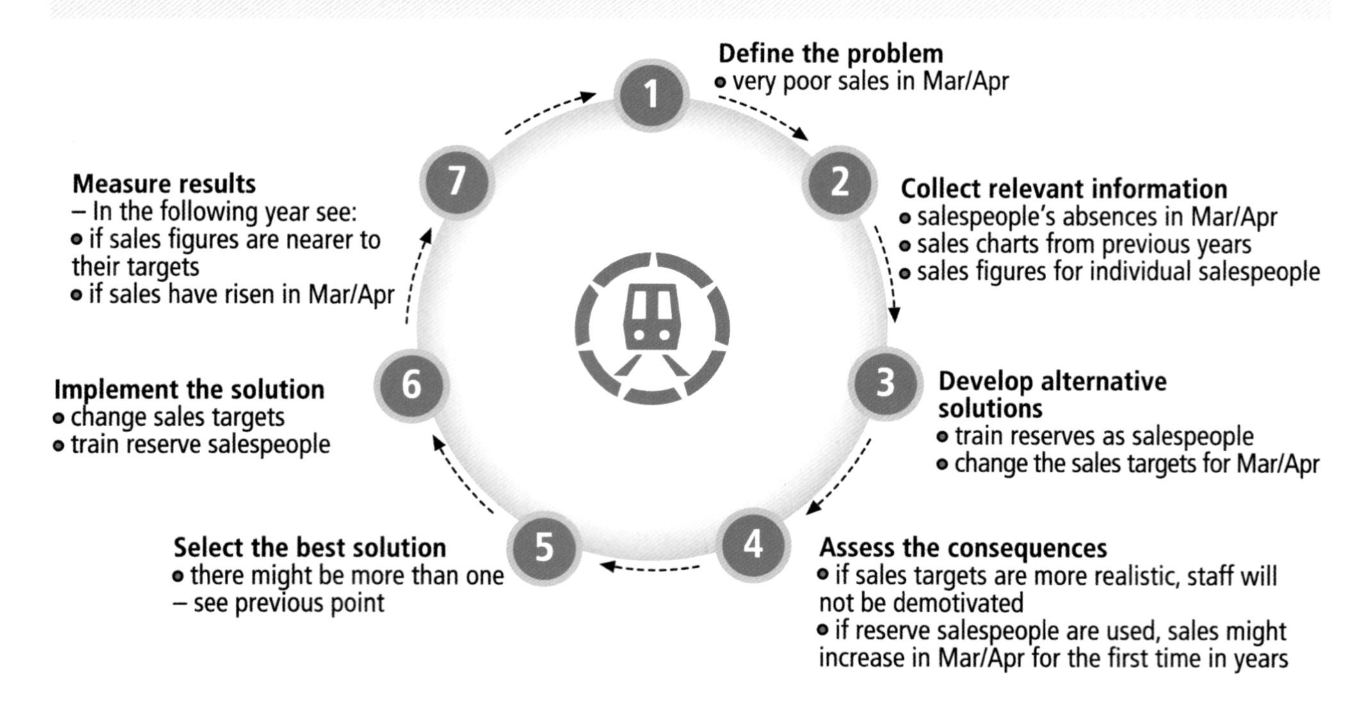

Questions 3

1 KiddiePix Ltd is a small business specialising in children's portrait photography. It is responsible for the product from the photography to the framing of the picture.

a Sales targets have not been met. Which source of information in Mary Birst's office shows this?

b Mary has decided that, as a result of sales targets not being met, she must replace one of her sales staff.

(i) State which one you think she will choose, and why. **DM**

(ii) What information source do you think she would base her decision on? **DM**

c External information has encouraged Mary to think that business will greatly improve very soon.

(i) Name two external sources of information which are shown in the picture.

(ii) State what information is contained in each source given in part (i) and state why they have made Mary more optimistic about business. **DM**

d Mary receives this memo from her photographer, James Grant.

MEMORANDUM
To: Mary
From: James
Subject: Full-time assistant

We are in danger of losing customers.
A backlog of work has occurred due to lack of staff.
We need another photographer immediately.

(i) Is the memo is an example of internal or external information?

(ii) Do you think Mary should consider employing another photographer soon? **DM**

(iii) State which information sources, shown in the picture, helped you to make your decision in **d** (ii) and say why. **DM**

Different management styles

Autocratic style

An autocratic management style occurs when managers tell people what to do and expect their orders to be followed. There is little or no consultation between management and workers in this regard. Decision making is tightly controlled.

Democratic style

A democratic management style means that managers consult others before making decisions. This could involve a senior manager discussing an issue with junior managers. It could also involve managers asking other workers for their opinions before reaching decisions.

Laissez-faire style

A laissez-faire style (French for 'let it be') involves the minimum of managerial direction. It probably works best in workplaces where creativity would be stifled by strict managerial control (e.g. designers). It does not mean that people can do exactly what they like at all times, however!

Impact of management styles on morale and motivation

Autocratic style

Workers in some businesses run in an autocratic style might feel frustrated and unable to use their initiative. This is likely to lead to low morale and little motivation. However, in some organisations (such as the Army) this style of leadership is felt to be vital. In moments of stress, armed forces are expected to follow their leaders without question. They are trained to respond positively to this management style, and clear leadership in this case is likely to increase motivation and morale.

Democratic style

If carried out properly, a democratic style should make workers feel part of the decision making. They will feel that their ideas are important and are acknowledged.

It is important, however, that they see it in this way. If they feel managers are approaching them for ideas because they have none of their own, this will lead to lack of respect and a perception of poor leadership. This will have a negative effect on morale and motivation.

Laissez-faire style

Laissez-faire management is quite relaxed which will not work in all industries. Most workers need clear leadership and guidance. In creative industries (e.g. advertising and film making) where creativity should not be stifled, this type of style may work well.

Style	Advantages	Disadvantages
Autocratic	The decisions that are made are often quick and decisive	Staff are not consulted, so may feel frustrated and disempowered
Democratic	Decisions are made in consultation with staff, so staff feel involved and are more likely to implement decisions	Consultation may take time, so decision may not be made quickly enough
Laissez-faire	Relaxed working environment works well for certain industries, especially creative ones	The organisation can sometimes lack direction

Effective management

Qualities of effective leadership

Effective leaders and managers have the following skills and qualities:

- good interpersonal skills, enabling them to lead, organise, motivate and work with their staff
- good informational skills, enabling them to communicate clearly, and collect, process and analyse information
- good decision-making skills, enabling them to use information to make different kinds of decisions.

Roles of a manager

Leading

Leadership is an important part of management. This can involve leading by example, giving clear instructions, and persuading and directing people. It is important to gain respect from the staff. A firm knowledge and understanding of the business and its practices help here.

Planning

Planning involves looking ahead and deciding what the future goals of the organisation are. Once these have been decided, plans must be made to help achieve these goals. Many organisations plan several years ahead.

Budgeting

Budgeting is a form of financial planning. Managers must be able to forecast the financial needs of an organisation, and show how these needs will be met. A budget is a forecast of future income and expenditure. If expenses are likely to be higher than income for a time, the organisation must either plan to cut costs, increase prices or obtain short-term loans. If income is likely to be much higher than expenditure, managers might plan to expand the business, reward the workforce, or improve premises.

Controlling

Managers should have a thorough knowledge of what is happening in their organisation. They should maintain control over the way the business carries out its activities, and ensure that the aims are being achieved. They should use their authority to make sure the correct procedures take place.

Monitoring and evaluating

Managers need to monitor or keep track of the activity of the business and the performance of staff, in order to compare them with targets and forecasts to see if these plans are being met, that is, if the business is on track. By making such evaluations managers will see if areas of the business are under- or over-performing and will be able to take decisions to address any problems. Failure to monitor will mean that managers probably won't identify small problems soon enough to prevent them from becoming big problems.

Questions 4

1 Different management styles are shown in the following descriptions.

(C)

Memorandum

To: All Sales Staff

From: Sales Manager

Decisions must be left to J Green, Sales Manager.

(D)

Memorandum

To: All Managers

From: Managing Director

A decision must soon be made about moving to other premises. All views will be welcomed at the meeting next week.

a State whether you think the management style shown in each picture is democratic, autocratic or laissez-faire.

b (i) State one way in which a democratic management style can help motivate staff.

(ii) How might an autocratic management style demotivate some staff?

(iii) In which two of these businesses do you think a laissez-faire style would probably work well: advertising; car manufacturing; dress design; supermarket; oil production? Give a reason for your answer.

2 Effective management involves **planning**, **budgeting**, **controlling**, and **monitoring and evaluating**. Use each of these terms as headings and write a paragraph on each of these management roles, showing what each involves.

Purpose of communication

Communication is an important part of management. Clear leadership and direction cannot be given if managers' wishes are not conveyed to the appropriate people within the organisation. Businesses also communicate to inform the outside world of their products or services in order to sell them.

Methods of communication

Written communication

A football club might use the following types of written communication, with each being useful to management in different ways:

- match tickets – help control crowd numbers, contribute to profits, record crowd numbers to help with future planning
- letters – help management to communicate formally with outside agencies, copies can be kept as a record – electronically or as hard (paper) copy
- memos – the information is recorded (electronically or on hard copy), and is less likely to be forgotten by those receiving them
- leaflets – useful for advertising and promotion in many different forms
- financial reports – these can be compared with those of other clubs and with previous years' performances, helping planning and budgeting; also used as information for shareholders.

Spoken (oral, verbal) communication

A football club conveys information verbally in the following forms:

- TV/radio interviews
- telephone conversations
- announcements at matches
- videos and DVDs.

Verbal communication is often immediate (as in match announcements) and can be received by large numbers of people at once. This can be a very cost-effective way of conveying information to a wide audience.

In the case of TV/radio interviews, videos and DVDs there will be a record of the communication. However, it is unlikely that records of telephone conversations and match announcements will be kept. The taping of telephone conversations is strictly controlled by law.

Visual communication

Visual communication is information which is presented graphically or pictorially, and includes:

- graphs and charts
- billboards
- video and film.
- posters
- photos

The visual nature of the communication is an important part of the message, and the presentation makes the message easier to understand and/or remember. Sometimes it might be attractive and appealing, sometimes it might simply present data, sometimes it might be striking or even upsetting.

Other types of communication

Internal and external information

Internal communication takes place within a business. Examples include:

- memorandums
- intranet
- loudspeaker systems
- internal telephone systems
- email
- bulletin boards
- mass storage devices such as pen drives, hard disks, etc.

External communications occur between a business and the outside world. Examples include:

- world wide web
- press releases
- notices/advertisements
- computer disks
- teletext
- letters
- videoconferencing
- CD-ROMs.

Formal and informal communication

Informal communications are casual in nature. They are often communicated to a small number of people. Examples include chatting by the water cooler (the office grapevine) and messages left on sticky notes. The information is usually valid only for a short period of time.

Formal communication is official in nature. It is usually in good quality print and the information will often be valid for a year or more. It includes sales reports, published annual accounts, and notices to all staff. It is often communicated to a large number of people.

Using ICT to communicate

ICT (information and communications technology) includes the internet, satellite communications and all types of telecommunications. These are often interlinked. Most managers now use ICT for the following reasons:

- speed of transmission, speed of accessing information
- cost-effectiveness
- to keep abreast of competitors
- to reach worldwide markets – using world wide web, email and satellite links
- to facilitate communications with customers (e.g. efficient phone systems and 24-hour computer links)
- efficiency in the maintenance of important records.

The main ICT methods of communication

ICT systems are very varied. They include the following:

- databases
- CD-ROMs
- satellite
- pagers
- spreadsheets
- memory sticks
- video conferencing
- word processing applications.
- internet
- expert systems
- phones

All of these can help with recording and generating information in order to aid decision making.

Advantages and disadvantages of using ICT to communicate

Advantages	Disadvantages
Speed and accuracy, saving labour Inexpensive to run Can communicate efficiently with many people at the same time Reduces waste Improves access to information Can improve communication and decision making	Can be expensive to install new equipment and train staff Data can corrupt, affecting productivity and communication Systems can break down, causing problems with communication flow and work flow Specialised ICT support required

For most forms of communication using ICT a consistent disadvantage is the potential for technology to fail or break down (whether hardware or software), causing inconvenience to those using it, and affecting productivity and work flow. Another disadvantage is the need for staff to be trained adequately to use the technology efficiently and competently.

Businesses must be careful to ensure that their ICT systems are fully secure and cannot be accessed by unauthorised people, or by those who may wish to cause malicious damage (hackers). Any business conducting e-commerce (financial transactions on the internet) must additionally ensure that the confidential data of customers (bank account, credit card details, etc.) is kept secure to prevent fraud resulting from unauthorised access by criminals.

Type of ICT	Advantages	Disadvantages
Word processing	Documents can be keyed in, stored and edited easily The appearance is professional, and multiple copies can be made easily Routine tasks can be done automatically (e.g. mail merge)	Not the best way to present numeric or graphic information Not ideal for the informal, personal touch, where handwritten work is better
Database	Many types of information can be stored and ordered easily, and the order can be changed in many ways Entire database can be printed, or extracts from it can be printed alone Can create reports efficiently	The accuracy of the data held in the database depends on the accuracy of the typing by operators
Spreadsheet	Can perform calculations in a routine way Worksheets can be linked so that data is updated automatically Can be used to create graphs and charts	Some training is required to know how to use and input formulae, especially with complex spreadsheets

Graphics packages	Can integrate images with text, creating more interesting and varied documents	Can be very complex to use and time-consuming to achieve desired layout Specialist staff might be required, which is costly
Email	One of the quickest, informal written forms of communication that (in some ways) is overtaking the fax machine Items such as photos and word-processed documents can be attached and sent	Can interfere with workflow Email needs to be checked regularly It is not a confidential way of sending information, nor is it a formal one It does not replace letters
Internet	Fast access to a vast market and a huge amount of information to people and businesses worldwide	Websites need to be kept up to date and secure People, and businesses, have to be wary when accessing, or giving, information and products from/to the web as security and safety issues are involved
Video-conferencing	Saves expense of travelling internationally to meetings	Not everyone is comfortable in front of a camera The equipment is not always efficient, leading to problems with sound and visuals
Mobile phone	Staff can be in contact when away from the office They are now very compact, easy to carry and many have access to the internet and radio	Not all regions have mobile phone coverage. There are restrictions on the use of phones (e.g. while driving, in hospitals and during air travel)

Choose appropriate ICT methods

Depending on the situation, different ICT methods might be more or less appropriate The following examples illustrate factors to be considered.

Example 1: Word-processing package or a database to create a table

Tables can be created using either a word processor or a database. When deciding which to use, the operator must decide what the table will be for, and how it will be used.

If it is a simple table, whose order is unlikely to change, or from which data is unlikely to be extracted in sections, then the word processor is better because it is quicker to set up and operate.

Using a database will be more appropriate, however, if the items in the table are likely to be added to, or deleted; if types of information are likely to be extracted or if the order of information is likely to be changed. It takes longer to set up a table in a database than using a word processor, but in the end the information can be changed and accessed more easily.

Example 2: Mobile phone or pager

If a pager is used, the person being paged must get access to a phone and call the appropriate person to find out what the message is. This is more time consuming than simply using a mobile phone. However, in hospitals a pager is more likely to be used because of the restrictions involved in using a mobile phone in hospitals (they can interfere with medical equipment).Therefore, the location and type of message being conveyed must be considered.

Evaluating communication methods

Managers should ensure the following with regard to communication systems in their organisation:

- that the appropriate method is used for each task
- that clear comparisons and evaluations are made regarding the effectiveness of different systems and methods
- that cost-effectiveness is achieved where possible.

For example, a sales manager has a hard copy (i.e. paper) of a 60-page sales manual. She also has a copy on memory stick. The sales manual is to be sent from Glasgow to London where it will be edited and sent back to her.

She can send this report in four ways.

Method	*Advantages*	*Disadvantages*
The hard copy is sent by post	Avoids possible problems of incompatible computer systems Some people prefer editing hard copies – they find them easier to read than screen versions	Could be costly Could be lost or damaged The sales manager will need to redo the edits on her computer
The memory stick is sent by post	The editing can be put straight on to memory stick, so is only done once	The memory stick could be lost or damaged
The report is sent by fax	Report is sent directly Less likelihood of damage or loss than by post Some people prefer editing hard copies	Time-consuming Costly The edits will have to be redone on disk later
The report is sent by email	The editing is done directly on the file, so is done only once Quick and cost-effective if the information is compacted*	There could be incompatibility problems Could be costly unless compacted*

* Sending many pages of information by email can take a long time and so can be costly in the same way that a long telephone call costs money. To avoid this, the information can be compacted or compressed using special software. This is the electronic equivalent of condensing a large pot of soup into a small tin can. The information therefore takes much less time to send.

Recommended decision

If the computer systems are compatible, and if the report is electronically compacted, the best method of communication would probably be email. This is because it is less expensive to send this document by email than by fax, and safer than posting it. If the report is edited on disk, the manager will not have to copy the edits back onto the original – the changes will be made immediately.

Effectiveness of different communication methods

A business may use different methods for different reasons when marketing a new product:

- phone – can contact many people very quickly
- email – as quick as the phone, but with the advantage of the written word
- letter/leaflet – better quality documents (e.g. glossy brochcures) can be sent by post
- TV/radio advertising – reaches a large number of people, but is expensive.

When launching a new product, a business may use some or all of these methods of ICT/communication. The method/s chosen will depend on cost, speed, range of people to be targeted, the type of product or service being launched.

TV advertising can target a lot of people, but there is little time to put over a large amount of information. When advertising a new car on TV, people are made aware of the existence and appearance of the car, and little else. A glossy brochure sent through the post (as back-up to the TV advert) can give more information like the size of engine, colours of paint available, range of prices, etc. Then a phone campaign could be the third stage of marketing activity, when potential customers are phoned to ask if they've seen the advert, if they've received the brochure, and whether they would like a test drive. This is an example of how different methods could be combined.

Emailing, phoning and sending letters are less expensive than TV advertising but are arguably less entertaining and may miss their targets. Many people have set up their phones and computers to stop marketing calls and emails from reaching them. Businesses must consider whether cost is more or less important than ease and success in accessing potential customers.
They must decide whether one or more methods should be combined.
The advantage of combining methods is that if some do not work, others might; or as shown in the car example, each method might add to the success of the one before.

Questions 5

1 **a** Why is clear communication important to the management of a company?

b Give three reasons why most managers now use information technology to help them communicate inside and outside their businesses.

2 The media uses a range of methods to communicate. For example, the BBC does not only use TV to communicate with its customers.

a List the other methods that the BBC uses, and the type of information and services it provides in each.

b State why you think the BBC uses this variety of sources and products.

ANSWERS TO QUESTIONS AND CASE STUDIES

Chapter 1 What is business?

Case study, pp. 9–10

1a Primary (extractive) industry.

b It involves the extraction of raw materials (fish) from nature.

2 Differences: sea fishing involves fishing for wild fish, so catches are not guaranteed; farmed fish are cultivated, so are easier to catch. Similarity: both sectors aim to sell the fish they have produced for a profit.

3 Sea (wild) fish include cod, plaice, langoustine; farmed fish include salmon, rainbow trout, cultivated shellfish.

4 Very important. It accounts for half (50%) of the Scottish food exporting industry; and three quarters (75%) of its jobs are in the Highlands and Islands.

Questions 1

1a Businesses in the public sector are owned and run by the state. Businesses in the private sector are owned and run by private individuals or groups of individuals.

b Needs: what people must have in order to stay alive, e.g. food and drink. Wants: include needs, but also include items which people simply like to have because they give satisfaction.

c (i) Production: the process of producing or making products, or adding value to raw materials.

(ii) Consumption: the purchasing and/or using up of items.

2a Sole trader b 20 c 50

d Any two points from: a small business is owned and run by a small number of people, whereas a large business is often owned by large numbers of shareholders and run by directors; a small business tends to sell goods and services locally, whereas a large one sells goods and services over a large area, sometimes worldwide; a small business employs fewer than 50 people, whereas a large one employs more than 250 people.

e Charity.

3a Forester (or any term that signifies the raw material stage of production), Sawmill, Furniture maker.

b (i) Private sector, tertiary sector.

(ii) Medium (it employs 50–250 people).

c 'Creating wealth' occurs at each stage of a production process. Value is added by each producer.

d Sawmill uses electricity, machinery and labour to convert trees into timber which is free from bark and dirt and is easier to transport and use. The cost of these processes adds to the value of the timber. The furniture maker adds screws, varnish, hinges and labour costs to the wood to make the table. The table is now usable.

Case study, p. 14

1a Shops such as Tesco, Next, etc. are likely to bring in more customers, which might bring more trade to the other retailers in the older parts of the town centre.

b Employment opportunities provide income.

2 Social cost.

3 It will help increase or establish incomes for some locals; this has the potential to increase local spending in the area.

4 Reduction in customers, and therefore revenue, during the building of the centre.

Questions 2

1a The willingness to turn an idea into a new product or service and finance it, or persuade someone else to do so; also the willingness and ability to take risks.

b Entrepreneur; examples include Linda Bennett and Richard Branson.

c Any three from: people do not want to buy the product or service; profits are not high enough to cover costs over an extended period; there is not enough cash flow for day-to-day expenses; more money is owed than can be paid back; all the money invested is lost.

d (i) Any suitable answer, e.g. Tesco, Sainsbury, ICI.

(ii) Public sector – any suitable answer, e.g. local council, hospital or school. Voluntary sector – any suitable answer, e.g. Oxfam, local youth club.

(iii) Tesco (or equivalent) – profit-making. Hospital (or equivalent) – providing a service for local people. It aims to break even, not to make a profit. RSPCA (or equivalent) – using donations to achieve its aims, that is, to look after abandoned and ill-treated animals.

(iv) Acceptable answers include: Tesco – customers who want good quality products and services at competitive prices; suppliers who want to be paid on time. Hospital – patients who want good health care; medical staff who wish to provide a good service. RSPCA – people who give donations want to know that their money is helping to look after animals; RSPCA inspectors want to provide a good service to animals and the public.

2 Any three stakeholders, e.g. Shareholders – to receive share of profits; Players – to win games and improve own financial success; Directors – are responsible for the overall business of the club, so its success is important; Media – need listeners and viewers as these generate money for media outlets; Local residents – those who live near a football club want minimum disruption in their area.

3a Social costs are negative effects on a community as a result of nearby businesses, e.g. pollution, heavy traffic, noise. Social benefits are improvements which take place in a community as a result of local businesses, e.g. better roads, improved housing, new schools.

b Economic costs are negative financial effects on a community, e.g. increased taxation, increased rates, increased cost of roads and other infrastructure. Economic benefits are positive financial effects on a community, e.g. increased income, extra spending which helps local shops, increased standard of living which helps individuals and businesses in an area.

Questions 3

1a (i) Tall structure.

(ii) Flat structure.

b (i) Tall structure has more lines of communication, and more levels of responsibility and authority, than flat structure.

(ii) Tall structure.

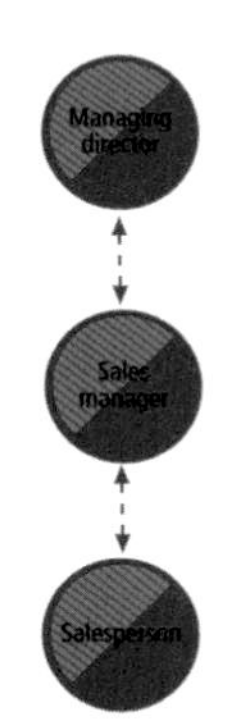

c Line relationships show who is directly responsible to whom in an organisation. The sales person is directly responsible to the sales manager who in turn is directly responsible to the managing director. The top of the line is the MD, so they have full authority over all the people below them. The MD also has full responsibility for the actions of all the people in the line below.

d 'Span of control' refers to the number of people under someone's authority. In a wide span of control those in authority supervise more people than those in authority in a narrow span of control.

e (i) When an area has a 'functional relationship' to another, it means it provides a direct service to it.

(ii) A Administration generally deals with administrative areas such as paperwork, reception, ICT. B Human resources recruits and looks after the welfare of staff.

f (i) Power or right to take a certain action.

(ii) Being answerable for actions/decisions. Note:Responsibility does not automatically bring authority but authority does automatically bring responsibility.

Chapter 2 How do businesses develop and perform?

Questions 1

1a B buyers; A seller.

b Any two, e.g. nobody would buy the games; she might have lost all of her money; Nasim might not be able to pay her expenses; she could have been forced to sell her house and car to pay off her debts.

c Any two, e.g. loan/overdraft from banks and other financial institutions; loans from family and friends; government grants; credit from suppliers.

d Any two e.g. government agencies; development agencies; partners; friends.

2a Buyers and sellers.

b Any four, e.g. outdoor market, shopping mall, high street shops, ice-cream van.

c (i), (ii) Land – water, trees, fields, oil, car parks; Labour – doctor, oil worker, lorry driver, teacher; Capital – factory building, shop, freezer; Enterprise – any two businesses which show enterprise as defined.

3a Desk research; field research.

b Desk research – studying secondary data (e.g. information from books, newspapers and/or the internet which already exists in easy-to-obtain form). It is quite often originally meant for another purpose. Field research – obtaining first-hand data straight from the market through surveys, questionnaires and/or phone calls. It is done for a direct (primary) purpose.

c Careful budgeting and planning can avoid the problem of not having enough money to pay expenses. This helps ensure in advance that loans and savings are sufficient to cope with expected (and unexpected) expenses. Careful market research should reduce the chance that a product will not sell.

4 a A business plan is an outline of a business, stating its objectives and how it plans to achieve these objectives.

b (i) A bank

(ii) To obtain a loan and other financial help, e.g. an overdraft

c Any five, e.g. General details about the business; Human resources; The product; The market; Premises/equipment; Profit estimates; Cash flow; Capital. Details of each area as described on page 25-26.

Case study, pp. 29–30

1 Any two, e.g. Since costs were going to be high, they had to be sure that they developed a suitable product, and that they matched it to the correct market; They had to test the suitability of different materials, which had to be tough and durable; They had to make sure that the product design was suitable for their requirements, with regard to safety, attractiveness and cost.

2 Any breach of safety on theme park rides is a major issue. No ethical organisation should take chances on this, for obvious humanitarian reasons. It could also be economically disastrous for the firm, damaging reputation and profits.

3 Any two, e.g. development of a scale model; choice and clearance of a site; building work; choice of name; advertising and promotion.

Questions 2

1a If one product or service fails, there will be other ranges of products and services which can keep the company going. The risks are spread.

b Any two, e.g. merger, takeover, internal diversification.

2a Creating new ideas and making new discoveries; creating new solutions for old problems.

b It allows the company to be first, provided it takes the idea forward and implements it. The company has a chance of maximising profit while competitors catch up.

c The best way to make discoveries is to look for them, which is what research and development departments do. Large pharmaceutical companies, e.g. Glaxo Smith Kline, employ large R & D departments to discover new medicines which can cure previously incurable illnesses; such discoveries can be very profitable.

3 Market research – researching the market and includes finding out what the market is (e.g. what age group or gender would buy the product). It also involves asking that market what it wants. Product research –: ensuring the product works; checking materials for quality and fitness for purpose; checking safety factors.

4a To increase profit; to achieve economies of scale; to spread risks by diversifying; to increase share of, and possible control of, the market.

b Economies of scale are the benefits a business obtains as it grows.

c External economies of scale are benefits from outside the business. Internal economies come from within the business.

Questions 3

1a March.

b Planning.

c Any acceptable term, e.g. cash budget; cash flow statement.

d Any two, e.g. bank overdraft; short-term loan of one year; extra credit from suppliers/creditors.

e It lets them know in advance in which months they will not have enough cash flow and they can plan ahead by asking the bank for an overdraft or loan as appropriate. This gives a better impression of control to a bank than a company which waits until a crisis strikes before asking for a loan. By then it might be too late.

2a Trading and Profit and Loss Account

b Net profit year 1 = £100,000; Net profit year 2 = £120,000

c (i) ratio = net profit / sales turnover x 100

Year 1: 100,000 / 250,000 x 100 = 40%

Year 2: 120,000 / 300,000 x 100 = 40%

(ii) The ratio has stayed the same. It is a reasonably good indicator, showing that profit per pound of products sold has stayed the same over 2 years, especially when it is quite a high ratio.

d Hatbox Ltd had greater sales than Bandbox Ltd, but both its gross and net profits were lower than those of Bandbox. This was because its cost of sales and its expenses were much higher than

Bandbox's. Management should seriously consider their trading costs. Perhaps they pay suppliers too much. The gross profit-to-sales ratio was 34% for Hatbox, while it was 60% for Bandbox. The net profit-to-sales ratio for Hatbox was only 9% compared to 40% for Bandbox. In both ratios, Bandbox's better figures show that it is much more efficiently managed.

3 Profitability – any two: Return on capital employed: net profit / capital employed x 100; Gross profit to sales: gross profit / sales turnover x 100; Net profit to sales: net profit / sales turnover x 100; Liquidity: Working capital ratio = Current assets : current liabilities; Efficiency: rate of stock turnover = cost of sales/average stock.

Case study, p. 41

1 They relied too much on one customer, and could not find enough business from elsewhere when M & S removed their custom.

2a It was cheaper. Wages cost less in some countries; this makes costs lower and profits expand, even if selling price remains the same.

b Since M & S were prepared to lower selling price, they became more competitive, while still maintaining a reasonable profit.

c They lost their jobs, and some found it difficult to get new ones in the textile industry. This was because many British clothing manufacturers were adversely affected by competition from abroad and their lower wages bills.

Questions 4

1 A 1; B 3; C 4; D 5

2 A 1; B 3; C 2

3a Any three, e.g. It does not reduce weekend rates, so the hotel lies empty at weekends. It charges higher prices for single rooms, so loses the custom of single travellers to the other hotels. It does not provide conference facilities, which are very profitable. Its systems are not computerised, so there are delays and cancellations.

b (i) Resources, such as labour, land and equipment, are not used efficiently and profitably.

(ii) Any three, e.g. The 'huge' grounds have not been used efficiently – parking facilities are needed but not provided; also a gardener could be employed to make them more attractive. Fabric of the hotel has not been properly looked after. The decor in the public rooms is described as 'having seen better days'. Staff are involved in time-consuming manual work, e.g. room bookings, which computers could handle more efficiently.

c (i) Any four, e.g. It could redecorate its public rooms; it could install a computer system for room bookings, appointments and accounts; it could employ a gardener to weed and care for the grounds; it could invest in a larger, new parking area; it could offer reduced rates for weekend packages and single travellers; it could offer conference facilities.

(ii) Any two, e.g. It could send leaflets to recent and/or regular customers; it could advertise in brochures and local newspapers; it could advertise on local radio or TV; it could erect a large notice in the grounds announcing the proposed changes and the dates of completion to passing traffic.

Questions 5

1a (i) Public sector – e.g. police, leisure centre run by the local authority, nationalised industries.

(ii) Private sector – e.g. Tesco, local supermarket, solicitors.

(iii) Voluntary sector – e.g. charities, clubs.

b (i) Any two for each sector, e.g. Public sector organisations measure success by: how successful they have been in providing the required products/services; how successful they have been in using their resources (i.e. labour, equipment and funding) properly; breaking even, i.e. not spending more than they receive. Private sector organisations measure success by: maximising profit; providing high quality products and services and keeping up with (or ahead of) their competitors; maintaining growth and a larger share of the market. Voluntary sector organisations often measure success in the same way as those in the public sector plus: providing the best services for their members (and/or beneficiaries in the case of charities; raising funding and achieving surpluses.

(ii) Yes – although there are some similarities.

(iii) The private sector consists of businesses whose main aim is usually profit maximisation. The main aims of the public and voluntary sectors focus on providing products and/or services for reasons other than profit.

2a Her main aim will be for the company to maximise profits so that she will receive maximum returns from her investment.

b Customers are often attracted by the lowest possible prices. This is often in conflict with the shareholder's wish for highest possible profits. Low prices can often mean lower profits.

c (i) Shareholders might receive fewer dividends in the short term. This might be caused by the high cost of making the required car park, which will cut profits in the short term. Customers might face higher prices to compensate the company for the cost of the improvements.

(ii) Poor environmental conditions due to exhaust fumes; danger for children crossing the streets; inconvenience to residents who cannot park near their own homes; traffic congestion in the streets.

Chapter 3 What resources do businesses use?

Case study, p. 47

1 Tesco Extra are much bigger than the Express stores; Tesco Extra provide clothes, food, electrical goods and a wide range of other products, whereas Express stores largely sell only food; Tesco Extra stores are usually out of town or on the outskirts, with large car parks whereas Tesco Express are in the centre of towns or petrol stations.

2 It competes against various sectors of the retail trade. It competes against large retailers like Asda on the edge of town with its Extra stores and superstores; against food retailers like M & S in town through its Metro stores; and against small convenience shops through Tesco Express stores.

Case study, p. 50

1 Yes, because the company would not get an RSA grant otherwise.

2 It does this because these areas have high unemployment and it wants to encourage firms there in order to create more jobs.

3 Yes; because it has created 20 jobs.

Questions 1

1a The nearness of a park means that people can sit and eat the ice cream. The nearness of a car park makes it easy for people to collect the ice cream and take it home. The school nearby will provide a ready market.

b He could take on a partner who could provide more capital. He could borrow money from friends or family, or from a bank or building society.

c Areas with high unemployment and industrial dereliction. The government wishes to reduce unemployment levels and make better use of land which is under-used. Crime rates are often linked to deprivation, which is another factor influencing the government.

d The EU gives grants to member countries, especially to areas which have high unemployment rates and have faced many factory closures.

e A multinational company has branches in many different countries. It usually starts trading in one country, but if it exports high numbers of products, there might be an advantage in producing products in other countries as well as selling them there. Nearness to markets, receipt of local government grants and low labour costs are factors which encourage multinationals to locate in various countries. Potential problems include communication/ language differences, time differences, legal and economic (including currency) differences.

2 Any four, e.g.government grant; bank loan; share issue (if it is a limited company or a plc and part of long-term expansion); EU funding.

3 Availability of raw materials – e.g. businesses which depend on bulky raw materials can reduce transport costs if they locate near to source of raw materials; producers which process perishable goods. Distance to market – e.g. local businesses who deal directly with customers; producers of fresh produce. Availability of labour – e.g. businesses which require many workers need to be located where the appropriate, qualified workers are available. Availability of land – e.g. large areas of land are required for farming; sporting events such as football and car racing, large flow production factories, such as car manufacturing. Transport costs tend to affect most businesses, although they will try to minimise these. Infrastructure (roads, railways, hospitals, colleges, utilities) also affects most businesses.

4a The European Union, which consists of 27 European countries, provides one market of over 490 million potential customers with very few, if any, restrictions between the member countries.

b Any three, e.g. No quotas between member countries – member countries can sell as many products to each other as they want. No customs duty between member countries. Free movement of workers and capital between member countries. Larger choice of suppliers. Makes high costs of research and development worthwhile since a business has a very large, unrestricted market in Europe. Increases competition which should increase efficiency. Procedures for moving products around Europe should be simplified. Restrictive practices (e.g. government subsidies and tariffs) are stopped.

c Any two, e.g. language barriers; distance problems; currency difficulties in the short term; bottlenecks in production due to large demand.

d (i) They enjoy the same large EU market as businesses from member countries, and avoid tariffs etc, which non-EU countries would normally face.

(ii) It brings employment, higher spending power and therefore a general increase in the standard of living and prosperity in depressed areas where these businesses set up.

Questions 2

1 Essential: Life-saving qualification, Driving licence, Enthusiasm, Excellent interactive skills, Punctuality, Ability to swim. Desirable: Previous experience, Ability to supervise a team, Some clerical skills, Knowledge of local area, First-aid certificate. Not relevant: Honours degree, Experience of working with animals.

2a Staff appraisal involves the evaluation by management of individual members of staff's performance, progress, strengths and needs in their jobs. Informal assessment is very subjective: it depends on the 'feelings' of the people appraising others, and is not based on agreed criteria. It is not usually discussed with staff. Formal appraisal is much more structured and usually involves the completion of a form, setting aside time for an appraisal interview, and appraising the person and/or job against definite criteria (such as quality of work, initiative and leadership skills).

b Sets targets agreed by both the appraiser and appraisee; recognises the employee's achievements; identifies difficulties; is objective; creates two-way communication between employers and employees or between managers and staff.

c (i) Positive feedback increases motivation; encourages employees to build on strengths; identifies training needs; helps identify promotion pathways.

(ii) Could increase workload; could cause the job specification to be altered; could be discouraging if not well handled.

d Target-setting involves the setting of time lines and making decisions on work to be achieved. It is important because it helps measure performance.

3a Any five (dates are not vital) e.g. The Disabled Persons (Employment) Acts 1944/58; The Factories Act 1961; Offices, Shops and Railway Premises Act 1963; The Equal Pay Act 1970; Contract of Employment Act 1972; Health and Safety at Work Act 1974; The Sex Discrimination Acts 1975/85; The Race Relations Act 1976; The National Minimum Wage Act 1998; Disability Discrimination Act 1995.

b (i) A written contract of employment.

(ii) Any four, e.g. job title and description, date the job starts, hours of work, rate and method of pay, holiday arrangements, period of notice that must be given when employment is terminated, pension scheme arrangements, rights concerning trade unions, details of the organisation's disciplinary procedures.

c Any four, e.g. Picketing – union members standing outside their own business's entrance, trying to persuade other workers not to go to work. Go-slow – workers deliberately slow down their work rate. Work-to-rule – workers follow the rules for their particular jobs strictly to the letter; they do no extra work, and the work is often slowed down by strict following of the rules. Overtime ban – workers refuse to work any extra hours over and above the hours in their contracts of employment. Strike – workers completely withdraw their labour for a period of time.

d Any two, e.g. Team working – employees are involved in setting targets, then gain recognition when these targets are achieved; working in teams, they participate in the decision-making process. Quality circles – employees pool their experience and specialist knowledge to study problems and suggest solutions. This helps create a feeling of worth and increases the motivation of the employees. Works councils – employees and managers work together to discuss working conditions.

Questions 3

1a Any four, e.g. list of phone numbers; memo pad on the desk; letters; telephone directory; road atlas; dictionary.

b Any three, e.g. information from the internet is shown on the computer screens; teletext on the TV; fax message; telephone; mobile phone.

c (i) Any three, e.g. memo; list of phone numbers; CDs.

(ii) Any four, e.g. phone book, road atlas, laptop, PC, fax, TV screen.

2a Which information is most important to them; what the information means; how it can be used to avoid problems in the future; how it can be used to ensure continued success

b Accounts – comparison of profits between years; comparison of profits with those of competitors; monitoring sales value and volume; checking for fraud. Worker performance – appraisals; employees' progress reports; sales volume and profits by department; customers' evaluations of workers. Production – targets; wastage; mechanical and technological reports.

Questions 4

1a Mechanisation – producing items, which were previously hand produced, with machines. However, workers are still required to operate these machines.

b Automation – many machines can now operate by themselves (automatically) with minimal supervision. Far fewer workers are required when machines are fully automated.

c (i) Unskilled jobs which included repetitive tasks.

(ii) Any two, e.g. increased output; increased labour productivity; increased quality; greater variety.

(iii) Automated cash machines in the high street and in shopping malls; phone banking services; Internet banking; debit cards.

d Governments have been putting more money into education and training. Businesses have also been investing in training staff.

2a If stock is lost or damaged, the business will lose money. Stock control must, therefore, be very accurate and closely monitored.

b Security, e.g. security staff and/or cameras, against internal and external theft is required. Record-keeping of amounts of stock ordered, amounts received and amounts sent out must be very accurate; computerisation helps. Accounting is very important in keeping track of costs – how much the stock costs will determine whether suppliers are used again and how much profit needs to be added on. Stock should not be stored for too long. Most products will deteriorate and/or go out-of-date if stored for too long. Also most businesses do not like to 'tie up' too much cash in their stock.

3a Poor quality products are likely to cause a fall in demand from customers and profits will suffer.

b (i) Quality control – inspectors check finished products and scrap items which are substandard. It can cause a lot of wastage because the defects are not identified until the products are complete, which is too late.

(ii) Quality assurance – this involves checking quality during and after production. It tries to stop defects occurring at all. The workforce is organised into teams which have the responsibility to make products to preset standards. This aims to ensure high quality work at all stages of production.

(iii) Total quality management is the most complete form of operations management. Everyone in the workplace is encouraged to think about quality in everything they do. It applies to all staff (not just those directly involved in production), including receptionists, sales managers and accounts personnel. Everyone aims to please the customer who should be at the heart of the whole process.

c (i) Just-in-time manufacturing involves ordering materials from suppliers just when they are needed for production. Very little or no material is kept in stock.

(ii) No stock is kept on the premises, so there is no need for warehouses and storage space. There should never be surplus or out-of-date stock.

(iii) If products at any stage of production are found to be faulty, workers and machines at the following stages will then have nothing to do. No more finished products will be produced until extra materials are delivered by the suppliers because no extra supplies or work-in-progress are kept in the factory.

Case study, p. 74

1 They feel that if they do not keep up with their competition they could lose out altogether. They have to react to competition by providing similar services, rather than simply stopping it.

2 They appeal to different markets. File swapping appeals in particular to younger people and to those with the relevant technology and knowledge. Not all people have access to this.

Questions 5

1a Poor industrial relations which could lead to industrial action (e.g. strikes and walk-outs); staff might become unmotivated, resulting in poor quality production; staff might leave and shortages occur – again production would suffer.

b (i) The costs of improvements might be very high and employers may be reluctant to pay these costs at first.

(ii) It is advisable in the long run because otherwise quality will suffer (due to poor quality premises and equipment, and unhappy staff who do not produce their best work). If quality suffers, demand from customers is likely to fall, and profits will fall.

c Internal.

2a The business will want to keep down costs, but internal pressures (such as security to monitor staff and equipment during activist demonstrations) and time restrictions (due to pressure from local residents) might cause difficulties in this area. Safety of staff and safety of equipment are important issues. It can be difficult to hire the appropriate staff within the required timescale. However, it is vital that the correct staff are employed for this type of project. Shareholders will, however, want high profits and this can be another internal pressure.

b Socio-cultural issues include: the need to minimise disruption to local residents. If people cannot get their cars out of driveways because of heavy construction equipment, relations between the business and the residents will quickly deteriorate. Legal requirements are also very important. If the business operates noisy machinery near houses at 1 am, this is likely to cause conflict between the company and legal bodies. Health and safety of workers as covered by law is another factor in such a project. Heavy machinery needs careful handling, and workers must be provided with safety clothes and gear.

Chapter 4 How are businesses managed?

Case study, p. 89

1 The new bar was introduced because the old KitKat design had been around for a long time, and its existing customers were ageing too. To interest a younger age group, researchers discovered that the product had to change.

2 Research investigated the types of product and packaging liked by the 18–25 age group.

3 No. Existing customers became interested in both the new and old bars, so existing custom did not fall away; it grew.

4 Possibly the maturity stage, before decline set in too badly.

Questions 1

1 What type of market research to use – field research, desk research or both; what questions to ask potential customers; whether to do the market research themselves, or employ an outside agency.

2 The type of product being made or service being provided; the type of jobs done – computers can replace some workers better than others; the availability of technology to do the job.

3 If higher profits could be made from the growth of the business; if demand for the product or service would be large enough to justify the extra cost of expansion; if growth would be the best way to compete with other businesses.

Case study, p. 94

1 If there is a demand for corks, cork forests will still be grown and nurtured, and this will be good for the continuation of wildlife such as the lynx. If demand falls, so will production and care of the trees, and this will mean less shelter and food for wildlife thus

threatening their existence. Secondly, trees are not cut down to extract cork.

2a The increase in use of screw tops in wine bottles.

b (i) Cork properties can sometimes damage wine.

(ii) Improvements in manufacture.

3 Portugal.

Questions 2

1a Customers' needs include: good-looking car, reliability, good price, low running costs, safety. Manufacturer's needs include: low costs, high profits, high demand. Competition from other businesses include: lower prices, attractive models.

b Social issues – Buyers in countries with good roads will have different requirements from those whose roads consist of dirt tracks. The living standards and social customs of potential customers can also affect the design of the car. Large families will have different requirements from small ones. Women drivers often have different requirements from male drivers. Legal issues – The new car must abide by the laws of the countries in which it will be sold. Most countries have strict laws about exhaust emissions and seat belt requirements.

c (i) Any two, e.g. interest rates; taxation levels; employment levels; value of the pound sterling.

(ii) Any two (which match the answers to part (i)), e.g. When interest rates are low, customers will be better able to obtain and afford loans to buy a car. When interest rates are high, not only is this not the case, but running costs will become much more important. Any car which has low running costs will be particularly attractive during a period of high interest rates. High income tax reduces people's spending power. High road tax and VAT add to the running costs of cars – which might affect the demand for new (and therefore relatively expensive) cars. When there is high unemployment, people might not want to buy new cars (choosing cheaper second-hand cars). This could make the manufacturer decide to postpone or cancel plans to produce a new model. When unemployment levels are low, demand for new cars might be higher – especially for second cars. The value of the pound sterling in comparison with the currencies of other countries makes imported cars more (or less) expensive.

(iii) Toll charges increase the general running costs of driving a car. If the car's initial price, servicing charges and other running costs are low, this will become more attractive to customers facing toll charges regularly. The manufacturer should take these things into consideration when deciding which design to use, which materials to use and which items are not essential to the car. Cutting costs without sacrificing safety is very important.

2a The candidates cannot be discriminated against on the grounds of race, sex or disability. The Race Relations Act 1976, the Sex Discrimination Act 1975 and the Disability Discrimination Act 1995 make this illegal.

b A contract of employment is a legal requirement. Every employee must be given a contract within 13 weeks of appointment.

Questions 3

1a The sales chart on the wall.

b (i) Bernadette – her sales commission is the lowest, so her sales must have been the lowest.

(ii) The sales commission list.

c (i) The internet, newspaper.

(ii) The internet shows that the FTSE is up 70 points and the newspaper shows that income tax has gone down by 30p in the pound. The first could indicate an increase in confidence in the economy which means people might spend more. An increase in spending power caused by a drop in tax will probably also mean that people will spend more, hopefully in Mary's business.

d (i) Internal.

(ii) Yes.

(iii) The information on the internet and in the newspaper indicate a favourable economic climate – which might result in more business. The accounts showing profits of KiddiePix and their competitors Pro Pics indicate that Pro Pics is not that far behind KiddiePix in profitability. KiddiePix therefore has to stay ahead and cannot afford to lose customers because of a backlog of work.

Questions 4

1a Democratic B, D; Autocratic A, C; Laissez-faire E

b (i) Workers are part of the decision making. They know that their ideas are important and are acknowledged.

(ii) Some workers can feel frustrated and unable to use their initiative, or to make much progress in the business.

(iii) Advertising and dress design. In both of these fields, too much direction from above could stifle creativity, adversely affecting the quality of the product.

2 Planning: involves looking ahead and deciding what factors need to be considered and dealt with for the future needs of the organisation. Budgeting: finances are a vital part of any business. Managers must forecast the financial needs of the organisation. A budget is a forecast of future income and expenditure for the business. If expenses are likely to be higher than income, the organisation can decide to reduce future costs, obtain a loan or increase income. Controlling: a manager should maintain control over the way a business carries out its activities so that the organisation's aims are achieved. She or he should know what is happening in the organisation and use her or his authority to make sure the correct procedures take place. Monitoring and evaluating: mean keeping track of how a business is progressing and how staff are performing. It is important that problems, no matter how small, are identified and solved quickly.

Questions 5

1a Managers cannot lead effectively if their wishes are not made known to other staff. Other staff must also be able to communicate information to their managers.

b Any three, e.g. for speed of transmission; for cost-effectiveness; to keep abreast of competition; to reach worldwide markets (e.g. by using satellite and internet); to facilitate customer communications (e.g. by using the phone); for efficiency in maintaining records.

2a Internet – a wide range of information is distributed through the BBC website including news, entertainment information, weather, and products available. This information can be accessed on mobile phones as well as computers. Radio – local and national news; local and national events; music; competitions. Books, videos and DVDs of BBC programmes.

b It uses this variety of sources and information to target as many people as possible, e.g. Radio 1 is aimed at younger listeners, Radio 4 at older, more serious listeners. It is also facing fierce competition from other TV and media providers and it is easier to compete if it provides a large variety of outlets for, and types of, its products and services. Since the BBC is funded by public money it must provide appropriate services to the British public and beyond. These services need to be appropriate for the modern consumers, many of whom can now access these via ICT such as mobile phones and computer.